T0222753

Windows Troubleshooting Series

Mike Halsey, MVP
Series Editor

Apress®

Windows Virus and Malware Troubleshooting

Andrew Bettany, MVP
Mike Halsey, MVP

Apress®

Windows Virus and Malware Troubleshooting

Andrew Bettany
York, North Yorkshire, United Kingdom

Mike Halsey
Sheffield, South Yorkshire, United Kingdom

ISBN-13 (pbk): 978-1-4842-2606-3
ISBN-13 (electronic): 978-1-4842-2607-0
DOI 10.1007/978-1-4842-2607-0

Library of Congress Control Number: 2017934653

Managing Director: Welmoed Spahr
Editorial Director: Todd Green
Acquisitions Editor: Gwenan Spearing
Development Editor: Laura Berendson
Technical Reviewer: Massimo Nardone
Coordinating Editor: Nancy Chen
Copy Editor: Michael G. Laraque
Compositor: SPi Global
Indexer: SPi Global
Artist: eStudio Calamar

Distributed to the book trade worldwide by Springer Science+Business Media New York, 233 Spring Street, 6th Floor, New York, NY 10013. Phone 1-800-SPRINGER, fax (201) 348-4505, e-mail orders-ny@springer-sbm.com, or visit www.springeronline.com. Apress Media, LLC is a California LLC and the sole member (owner) is Springer Science + Business Media Finance Inc (SSBM Finance Inc). SSBM Finance Inc is a Delaware corporation.

For information on translations, please e-mail rights@apress.com, or visit www.apress.com/rights-permissions.

Apress titles may be purchased in bulk for academic, corporate, or promotional use. eBook versions and licenses are also available for most titles. For more information, reference our Print and eBook Bulk Sales web page at www.apress.com/bulk-sales.

Any source code or other supplementary material referenced by the author in this book is available to readers on GitHub via the book's product page, located at www.apress.com/9781484226063. For more detailed information, please visit www.apress.com/source-code/.

Printed on acid-free paper

*Thanks, Mike, for your vision in creating this troubleshooting series.
I hope after reading this book, some readers will be saved
from the pain otherwise incurred by malware. Stay safe.*

—Andrew Bettany

*With many thanks to Grzegorz Tworek and the security researchers at CQure.pl
for providing a test virus, and for their help in making this book possible.*

—Mike Halsey

Contents at a Glance

Contents

About the Authors

Andrew Bettany has been a Microsoft Most Valuable Professional (MVP) since 2012, in recognition for his Windows expertise.

As a Microsoft Certified Trainer, Andrew provides expertise and consultancy services to businesses in a number of technical areas, including Windows deployment and troubleshooting.

He cofounded and manages the IT Masterclasses series of short technical courses, available at www.itmasterclasses.com, and is passionate about learning and helping others. He is also a frequent speaker at conferences worldwide. In 2011 and 2013, he delivered a training boot camp in earthquake-hit Haiti to help the community rebuild its technology skills.

Active on social media, Andrew can be found on LinkedIn, Facebook, and Twitter. He lives in a village just outside the beautiful city of York, in Yorkshire, UK.

Mike Halsey was first recognized as a Microsoft MVP in 2011. He is the author of more than a dozen books on Windows, including *Troubleshooting Windows 7: Inside Out, Troubleshoot and Optimize Windows 8: Inside Out, Beginning Windows 10, Windows 10 Troubleshooting* and *The Windows 10 Accessibility Handbook* from Apress. He is also the author of other troubleshooting books related to Windows in this series. Based in Sheffield, UK, where he lives with his rescue border collies, Evan and Robbie, Mike gives many talks on Windows subjects, from productivity to security, and makes how-to and troubleshooting videos under the banners PCSupport.tv and Windows.do. You can follow him on Facebook and Twitter at @PCSupportTV.

About the Technical Reviewer

Massimo Nardone has more than 22 years of experience in security, web/mobile development, cloud, and IT architecture. His true IT passions are security and Android.

Massimo has been programming and teaching how to program with Android, Perl, PHP, Java, VB, Python, C/C++, and MySQL for more than 20 years. He holds a master ofsScience degree in computer science from the University ofsSalerno, Italy.

He has worked as a project manager, software engineer, research engineer, chief security architect, information security manager, PCI/SCADA auditor, and senior lead IT security/cloud/SCADA architect for many years. His technical skills include security, Android, cloud, Java, MySQL, Drupal, Cobol, Perl, web and mobile development, MongoDB, D3, Joomla, Couchbase, C/C++, WebGL, Python, Pro Rails, Django CMS, Jekyll, Scratch, among others. He currently works as chief information security officer (CISO) for Cargotec Oyj.

He was a visiting lecturer and supervisor for exercises at the Networking Laboratory of the Helsinki University of Technology (Aalto University). He holds four international patents (PKI, SIP, SAML, and Proxy areas).

Massimo has reviewed more than 40 IT books for different publishing companies, and he is the coauthor of *Pro Android Games* (Apress, 2015).

Windows Troubleshooting Series

When something goes wrong with technology, it can seem impossible to diagnose and repair the problem and harder still to prevent a recurrence. In this series of books, we'll take you inside the workings of your devices and software and teach you how to find and fix the problems, using a simple step-by-step approach that helps you understand the cause, the solution, and the tools required.

Series Editor
Mike Halsey, MVP

As a Microsoft MVP (Most Valuable Professional) awardee since 2011, the author of more than ten books on Microsoft Windows, and a teacher for many years, Mike Halsey understands the need to convey complex subjects in clear and non-intimidating ways.

He believes that the Windows Troubleshooting Series is a great example of how quality help, support, and tutorials can be delivered to individuals of all technical ability. He hopes you enjoy reading this and many other books in this series, both now and for years to come.

CHAPTER 1

■ ■ ■

What Is Malware?

Few things can happen to a PC that are worse than it becoming infected with malware. As a consequence, your PC might fail to start, you may lose your connection to the Internet, or a hardware component in the PC might fail, but all of this pales into insignificance when compared to the threat of infection.

Why is this? While troubleshooting problems on PCs commonly leads us to discover that the problem is isolated to just the machine in question, malware infection immediately threatens not just every other PC on your network but your servers, storage (both local and cloud), clients, partners, employees, and much more besides.

With the introduction of ransomware in the last few years, the threat is worse than ever before. Businesses might suddenly find all their documents and files encrypted and a demand for payment of a large ransom for the decryption key.

It's not all doom and gloom though, as removing any type of malware from a PC, even unpleasant ransomware, is simpler than you might believe. Protecting your PCs from malware is even simpler still.

In this book, you'll learn about the different types of malware threats that can attack PCs and networks, how you can defend against and identify them, and, most crucially, eradicate them, should an attack occur.

A Brief History of Malware

This might come as a surprise, but the earliest computer viruses were written for the Apple II and Macintosh computers. They would write themselves into the boot sector of a floppy disk, so they would execute when the disk was read.

The popularity of the IBM PC and MS-DOS caused a boom in viruses, as computer use grew within businesses. Viruses were tiny in size, when compared to the malware of today, and typically performed small tasks, from deleting files to rewriting the PC's BIOS, so as to prevent the machine from starting, and then propagating further by copying themselves to every floppy disk placed into the machine. The first virus I was infected with, on an Olivetti PC back in 1991, played "Yankee Doodle Dandy" to me every day at five o'clock but was otherwise benign.

The Morris Worm was the first example of an Internet virus. Discovered at the end of 1988, it was written by a graduate student at Cornell University (Ithaca, New York) and launched from the computers of the Massachusetts Institute of Technology.

© Andrew Bettany and Mike Halsey 2017
A. Bettany and M. Halsey, *Windows Virus and Malware Troubleshooting*,
DOI 10.1007/978-1-4842-2607-0_1

Although it was not originally written to cause any damage but to gauge the size of the Internet for its creator, an error in its code turned it from a harmless worm into an infectious denial-of-service tool that took significant time to remove from the thousands of computers it infected.

Since then, there have been many high-profile viruses in the wild, including the infamous Stuxnet worm that was allegedly created by the US and Israeli intelligence services to infect Iranian government computers and report on the country's nuclear program. The Code Red worm of 2001, which defaced web sites and launched denial-of-service attacks, was at one point infecting more than 300,000 computers every day.

The rise of bots and ransomware took malware infection to a new level. A bot would infect thousands, sometimes even millions, of computers and then sit silently waiting for instructions. Control of the infected PCs would then be sold on the dark web to the highest bidder, who could then record keystrokes (such as usernames and passwords) from the PCs, get backdoor access to them, or launch distributed denial-of-service (DDoS) attacks that would flood Internet services and specific companies' web servers with so much traffic, and over such a prolonged period, that the servers would fail.

Ransomware, which encrypts the files and documents of individuals and companies, is widely reported to be raking in millions of dollars for its creators every year, as universities, hospitals, major corporations, and even governments secretly pay costly ransoms for unlock keys.

Today, malware exists on every computing platform and operating system. The popularity of Google's Android OS makes it a very tempting target, and even the advanced security of Apple's iOS and OS X systems offers no guarantee of protection, because, as I'll explain shortly, it's the user and not the software that's commonly attacked.

Internet of Things (IoT) devices are a new route of attack into your network or home, as they can often come with very lax, or even zero, security. Once connected to your network and your router, they can be used as gateways through which other devices can also be accessed. Often, physical access to the IoT device will be required to infect the device, though it's not unheard of for viruses to be pushed through firmware updating. If you use IoT devices, it's always wise to change the default administrator username and password and to check that the manufacturer has taken security seriously when designing the firmware.

For the purposes of this book, however, I'll be focusing on Windows 10 PCs and networks, which include servers, desktops, laptops, ultrabooks, and tablets, primarily running on Intel processors. ARM-based Windows 10 systems, such as smartphones and low-power devices, are less susceptible, because they are based on a more modern, and more secure, architecture of the Windows OS and don't include the "legacy" code and features that are often the focus of malware attack. They are, however, not completely immune, and as such, the same techniques I'll teach you in this book for removing malware from Intel-based systems will also apply to infections on ARM-PCs.

The Psychology of Infection?

There was a time before the Internet when every single PC was a stand-alone, individual machine and, as such, the security they had in place was often poor, or even nonexistent. Even when the Internet became widespread in the late 1990s, it took companies such as Microsoft many years to become fully aware of the threat poor security posed to their users and their reputations.

The problem with viruses arose because malware exploited security vulnerabilities in operating systems that would allow them to run—automatically, unhindered, and silently—when they arrived on a PC via an e-mail, infected file from a disk, or across a network. Therefore, operating systems such as UNIX and Mac OS, which was a UNIX derivative, were often hailed as being far more secure than their Windows counterpart, because the user of the PC did not have the administrative rights needed to allow malware to run.

These days, however, our Windows PCs are far more secure. Features such as User Account Control (UAC), first seen in Windows Vista, and Secure Boot, introduced with Windows 8, offer valuable first-line protection against infection. For this reason, the criminals (now more often criminal gangs) behind malware began to look to psychology to propagate their code.

How could end users be tricked into installing their malware? The answer was to disguise the malware as something innocuous, useful, or even fun, such as a codec required to play video on a web site, or an app, OS update, or driver that you might normally download directly from the official provider but that has been modified with an added payload and then made available on file-sharing or popular download sites.

The first line of defense against malware these days must be education and training of PC users, be they at home or in the workplace. People might find a "funny cat" video that won't play without the codec being installed, a game that one of their colleagues has been playing, or they might be tired or rushed and click a security notice without first reading it or paying attention to what it might mean.

Any granting of administrative rights to malware allows that malware to install and operate freely on the PC. Even if something looks like a legitimate or fun game, it could have an unpleasant payload in the background, operating silently against you.

In the business space, and especially with ransomware, the problem is exacerbated. It takes only one employee (or perhaps a student at a university), overworked and up against a tight deadline, clicking a UAC security prompt, so that she can open a file a colleague or friend has sent her, to give malware free reign to access any resource then available to that user on the network.

Criminals take advantage of the fact that the average PC user is not a technically minded person who understands, or even has to understand, how an operating system and software work and what a malware infection is capable of doing. It's the same issue people face with their personal and banking details. Only when someone's credit card details are stolen might he begin to re-evaluate covering his hand when he types his PIN at an ATM or in a shop or creating a more secure password for himself.

The two main defenses against malware infection, therefore, have to be preventing users from being able to run code or install software and, in such cases where it is difficult or simply impossible to achieve this, to educate PC users on the threat of malware, how it propagates, and the types of things it is and is definitely not acceptable for them to click.

Different Types of Malware

You might have noticed so far in this book that I've been referring to the terms *malware, worm,* and *virus* almost interchangeably. This is because there are many different types of malware (which is an umbrella term) that can affect PCs.

Viruses and Worms

Viruses and worms are the best-known types of malware, and they're named, not for the actions they perform, but for the way they propagate. A virus, for example, will spread from one machine to another through a medium comparable to that of a virus that you might catch in your own body, such as physical contact or sharing. A worm, however, will burrow from one machine to another via a network. Viruses and worms may perform one or more of the actions described in the rest of this section.

Spyware

Privacy is one of the buzzwords of modern computing, as social networks and major corporations collect data and information about our activities online, where we go (both physically and online), what we look at, what we buy, who our friends are, and what they like, etc.

Spyware is malware that performs these tasks independently of a connection to a specific social network or web site. Spyware will gather information about what you do offline and online on your PC and send that information, which can include recording keystrokes you type when you sign into web sites, online shops, and banks, using a keylogger, back to its creators.

Adware

Adware is the most innocuous type of malware, being something that is intended to display ads to you on your PC. These will commonly come in the form of pop-up windows, in a browser or separately. There is no real threat from adware, unless it also carries an additional payload, such as a keylogger.

Trojans

A Trojan, also known as a Trojan horse, is a package that is intended to appear completely innocuous and harmless but contains a hidden payload. It is named for the wooden horse the Greeks gave as a gift to the citizens of the city of Troy about the 12th century B.C. that contained soldiers who opened the city gates at night, allowing an invading Greek army to overpower the local inhabitants. So, technically, it was a Greek horse, and not a Trojan horse, but we'll skip lightly over that bit.

Trojans will typically appear as audio or video codecs (plug-ins required to play a music or video file or view a video online), a web browser plug-in, a game or something otherwise amusing or useful, or a pirated app, an ISO disk image installer for an operating system, or a document.

Bots

Bots are usually for sale. If you hunt around a little on the dark web (which I don't really recommend), then among the drugs, weapons, and other illegal goods that are sold there, you'll probably find something called a "botnet." Botnets are networks of machines that are infected by bots.

Typically, a bot will use the Internet connection of the infected machine to launch a prolonged DDoS attack on a company or web site. All the end user will notice is a slowdown in his/her Internet speed, but with thousands, perhaps tens or hundreds of thousands, of bots available and online at any one time, botnets can be an effective way for criminals to extort money from companies, or for political groups (and occasionally even governments) to attack a country's infrastructure.

Rarely, however, will bots be used merely for this single task. They will almost always include keyloggers and control software that offers backdoors into the PCs they have infected.

You'll occasionally hear about companies such as Microsoft taking down a botnet, usually with the help of a security company (or more), and always with the help of local law enforcement officials in the relevant territories. When a network such as this is taken offline, a common criminal activity, usually the sending of spam, can temporarily fall by up to a third on a worldwide basis, such is the prevalence of bots across the globe.

Such takedowns are possible because companies such as Microsoft, Apple, and Google, which provide the base OS, are well-placed, through the anonymous reporting they receive from their operating systems, to identify botnets, and, by using network traffic data and by reverse-engineering the bots from infected machines, they can trace the IP addresses, and the individuals, controlling them. This is all done without compromising users' privacy and always within the law.

Rootkits/Bootkits

When Microsoft launched the Windows 8.1 operating system, it mandated that all new PCs sold with the OS on board have the modern UEFI firmware on the motherboard, with Intel's Secure Boot system enabled.

Secure Boot is intended to defend against rootkits and boot sector viruses (bootkits) from infecting PCs. These malware types will embed themselves deep into the boot partition(s) on a PC. The rootkit will then start the OS in a hypervisor-type environment, which will give it complete control of the OS, while at the same time hiding and shielding itself from any security software you have installed and any security features in the OS itself.

A rootkit will commonly exploit OS features, such as the ability to install extensions into an app or by hooking into or patching an application programming interface (API) that contains an exploitable vulnerability. Once compromised, the rootkit can gain control of the application's execution flow and use its permissions and privileges to attack the PC's security and boot systems. It is partially because rootkit infections, which store apps in all operating systems, and Win32 apps, installed either from the Windows Store or on an ARM-based PC, run in their own protected areas of memory.

Rootkits and boot sector viruses can be extremely difficult to remove, given that they reside in hidden and protected partitions on the disk, and extremely difficult to detect.

You might think that if you have Secure Boot enabled on a PC that you'd be immune from rootkit attacks. Sadly, this isn't the case, as some vulnerabilities do exist within the Secure Boot system that can still allow rootkits to install. Additionally, some operating systems, such as Linux and Windows 7 will not start if Secure Boot is enabled, as they do not support the signed security that Secure Boot looks for at startup, which authenticates the OS as being genuine. All of this means that PCs running unsigned operating systems, in either a single or dual-boot scenario, must have Secure Boot disabled.

Backdoors

I've already alluded to backdoors several times in this section, as they are commonly part of the payload of a bot or other malware type. Backdoors permit remote access to, and sometimes remote control of, an infected PC. This will give criminals (and sometimes security agencies and governments) file, folder, and document access to a PC and any file shares and other PCs and servers on the network(s) to which it is connected.

Ransomware

By far the most unpleasant malware is ransomware. This malware will encrypt your files and documents (sometimes even more than these) and demand that you pay a ransom, usually in the online currency Bitcoin, for the decryption key.

As we store more and more files on network shares and in the cloud, and our PCs have access to these storage areas, and other network-connected PCs, ransomware is not only able to encrypt file backups but can also spread to other machines on the network and employ the user access permissions on those PCs to access yet more storage areas and more PCs. Some ransomware will even encrypt an entire disk in a PC, or the master file table (MFT) on the disk that contains the directory of what files are to be found where on the disk.

It is well known that hundreds of universities, hospitals, companies, and even governments around the world pay ransoms every year, so as to avoid the costly downtime required to rebuild the infected systems and losing critical files and data. These companies and organizations, however, will almost never publicize what has happened, because of the negative effect it can have on their reputation and the uproar from people whose private information has been compromised.

It is also well known that the decryption key, should you pay the ransom, will itself contain an additional malware payload. The criminals behind ransomware, however, are clever enough not to price their ransoms too high, as the financial benefit of an individual, business, or organization not being able to afford the ransom will not bring in revenue to the criminals. This, sadly, then creates an incentive for people to pay the ransom when they become infected.

Spam and Phishing E-mails

Spam (unsolicited) and phishing e-mails (e.g., purporting to be from your bank or a shopping site), an example of which is seen in Figure 1-1, aren't malware, but I'm including them here, as they can commonly lead to a malware download. Spam is named after the processed meat (pork shoulder meat and ham) that was a common foodstuff in the United States and United Kingdom during and after the Second World War, when food rationing was in place. It was widely disliked and derided (perhaps most famously in the Spam song by Monty Python) and was, therefore, a good choice of name for unwanted e-mails that began to appear in people's inboxes.

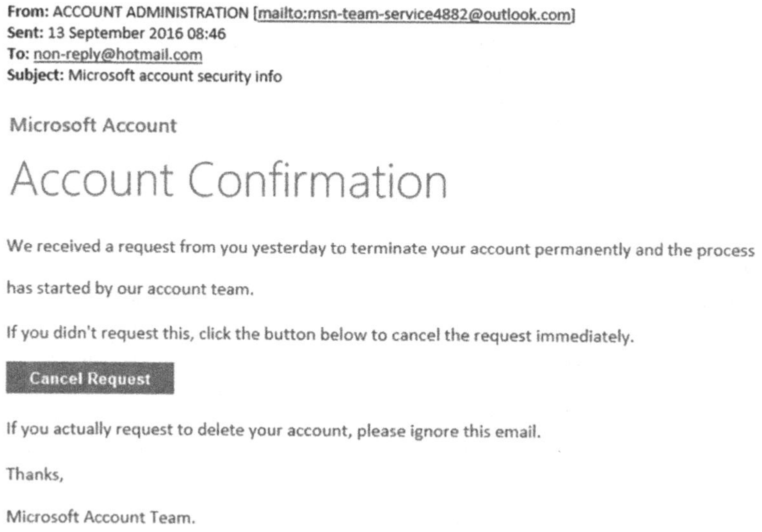

From: ACCOUNT ADMINISTRATION [mailto:msn-team-service4882@outlook.com]
Sent: 13 September 2016 08:46
To: non-reply@hotmail.com
Subject: Microsoft account security info

Microsoft Account

Account Confirmation

We received a request from you yesterday to terminate your account permanently and the process

has started by our account team.

If you didn't request this, click the button below to cancel the request immediately.

```
Cancel Request
```

If you actually request to delete your account, please ignore this email.

Thanks,

Microsoft Account Team.

Figure 1-1. *Phishing e-mails can be extremely convincing*

The Future of Malware

Clearly, malware is an enormous threat to our PCs, our files, data, and personal information. All of the preceding have a value, be it a value to yourself, in which case you will pay to regain access to it; a value to criminals, in that they can sell it or sell access to it; or even a value to governments and political/paramilitary/terrorist organizations, in that they can use it to disrupt the infrastructure of an adversary.

There's even a term to describe this type of attack, *cyberwarfare*, and examples of this have already been seen in the massive hack against Sony Pictures Entertainment in 2014, which was largely attributed to the company releasing an unflattering film about the North Korean leadership, though this was never proven, and attacks on secretive government security agencies, oppressive governments, and companies evading taxes, by the hacking group Anonymous.

The next war will be fought online, of which many people have little doubt. The ability to disrupt financial markets, communications, electricity and gas generation and distribution, traffic flow, shipping and aircraft, GPS satellites, health systems, government operations, or even military forces is hugely appealing to a great many people worldwide. That's why every year thousands of "white hat" hackers meet at DEF CON conferences, with representatives of corporations, technology firms, and security agencies from around the world, to discuss the latest vulnerabilities, threats, the malware incident handling process, whereby information can be shared between companies and security vendors in a secure way, and to find ways to mitigate against them.

If you think your PC isn't safe today, then don't get too disheartened, because you also have to worry about hacking and malware attacks on your car, home automation kit, and even essential medical devices, such as heart pacemakers. The list includes anything containing silicon chips and that runs some form of operating system. All we can ever do is keep people as educated as possible, and do what we can to defend against both the attack types we know of and the ones that we don't.

Ransomware, as an example, was only devised recently, and we can be certain that in the future, we'll face additional malware infection types that we can't imagine or envisage today.

Summary

If all of this isn't scary enough to make you want to dispose of all your technology and retreat to a small cabin deep in the woods, then fear not.

This is just one of six chapters in this book, and the other five are devoted entirely to defending against, identifying, and removing malware in all its forms. So, press on from here, brave traveler, and don't have nightmares, because it's how you can prevent malware infections in the first instance that I'll cover in the next chapter.

CHAPTER 2

■ ■ ■

Prevention and Defense

I stated in the previous chapter that there are two main things that you can do, as an IT professional, to defend your systems against malware. One is to make it as difficult as possible for users to install malware on your systems or to transfer malware-infected files onto your storage servers. This is achieved by using a combination of technologies, processes, and strategies that together can make malware infection difficult.

The other is to train staff in the different types of malware threat, how they are spread, how to spot them, and what it is and isn't safe to click and permit. This is called security awareness, and it should be a staple of all training for employees in any business or organization.

It's not always possible, however, to block users from performing actions such as installing software, and it certainly isn't possible to prevent users from moving files around, saving them from e-mails and copying them from and to USB flash drives. This is where configuring good preventative measures on your PCs becomes essential, as the PC itself then becomes the first line of defense against any malware.

Microsoft Windows comes with a multitude of tools for defending against malware, though the features on offer do vary from one version of Windows to another, with, as you might guess, the best suite of security tools available in the most modern version of the OS. I want to look at each of these tools in turn, but first I'll detail just what you can find in each different OS version (Table 2-1).

Table 2-1. *Security Features Available by Windows Version*

Tool	Windows 7	Windows 8.1	Windows 10
Security Center	X	X	X
Windows Defender	Download	X	X
Windows Defender Offline	Download	Download	X
Windows Firewall	X	X	X
Windows Firewall with Advanced Security	X	X	X
User Account Control	X	X	X

(continued)

© Andrew Bettany and Mike Halsey 2017
A. Bettany and M. Halsey, *Windows Virus and Malware Troubleshooting*,
DOI 10.1007/978-1-4842-2607-0_2

Table 2-1. (*continued*)

Tool	Windows 7	Windows 8.1	Windows 10
SmartScreen		X	X
Malicious Software Removal Tool	Option	Option	X
Secure Boot		X	X
Trusted Boot		X	X
App Containers		Limited	X
Early Launch Anti-Malware		X	X
Mandatory Security Updates	Option	Option	X

Organizational-Level Security

Before I jump into detailing the security tools and features of the Windows OS itself, it's important to discuss malware prevention on an organizational level. This includes the strategic plan for how all aspects of a business or organization handles security. The considerations that have to be made include the operational, tactical, and strategic security activities that will affect every PC, server, network system, and mobile device in the organization, as well as how bring your own device (BYOD) and guest devices are treated.

Additionally, these security strategies cover the rules governing how data is guarded and transferred across and outside the company network. You may, for example, have a policy that no company files should be transferable to a removable storage device, such as a USB flash drive, DVD, or guest laptop.

Staff security awareness training is also an essential component in an organizational security strategy, as the people using the computers in any business or workplace are always the weak link where security is concerned.

Having an organization-wide security strategy can assist considerably in the prevention of malware, because, let's not forget, in the age of the Internet, there really is no such thing as a stand-alone PC or isolated network anymore.

Core Microsoft Security Features

The security features in different Windows versions fall into different categories, depending on the type of support and security they offer. At the forefront of this are core features that exist across all supported versions of the OS. The Microsoft security web page, accessible at http://pcs.tv/2iCD4pF, contains up-to-date information on threats, prevention, and defense, as well as information on subjects such as legal compliance, transparency, and privacy.

Security Center/Security and Maintenance

The *Security Center,* called *Security and Maintenance* in Windows 10, is most prominent in Windows versions 7 and 8.1, where it sits in the system tray behind a little white flag (the irony of which has never been lost on me). It's the Security Center that will automatically, and periodically, check for problems with Windows Update and the network, firewall, and troubleshooting settings, and report to you if a problem is found.

It is designed as a central location for getting information about the status of the security on your PC (see Figure 2-1). There are collapsible panels for Security and Maintenance, and alerts are highlighted with traffic light colors, including green when everything is fine, amber if you should be aware of something that isn't urgent, and red for a critical alert, such as Windows Update or your antivirus updates being out of date.

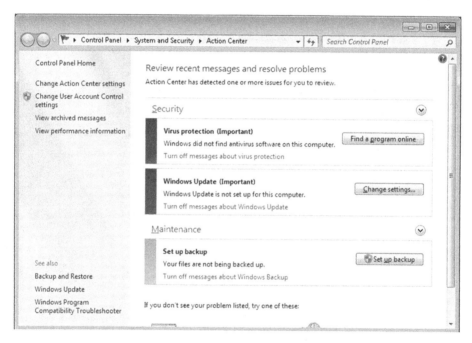

Figure 2-1. *The Windows Security Center*

User Account Control

User Account Control (UAC) is a security subsystem that acts as the first line of defense against any malicious software installations and unwanted OS system changes. It is accessed through the Security Center or by searching for "UAC" in the Start menu. Any user wanting to change UAC settings will first have to have administrative permissions on the PC.

The feature displays an alert dialog in the secure Windows environment that's used to display the sign-in dialog. In this special environment, nothing can be done with the OS except interact with the single dialog that's displayed, and only the user can do that, as all background processes are suspended. This means that malware cannot hijack the screen and click through the prompt itself.

There are four separate settings for UAC (see Figure 2-2) that begin at Never notify, which will turn UAC off completely, through to Always notify, which I like to call "Annoying Mode." The default setting for UAC will notify you when changes are being made to the PC that will affect all or other users on the machine (whether there are additional user accounts or not), which include disabling features, installing an app, and accessing a core system folder, but not changes that would only affect your own account, such as modifying your language settings or setting the correct time. I'll cover UAC in more detail in Chapter 3.

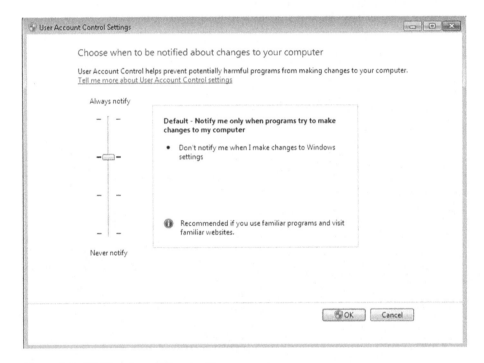

Figure 2-2. *UAC has four different settings*

Windows Firewall/Advanced Firewall

Windows comes with two different firewall interfaces: the default firewall and the advanced firewall. I won't go into these in too much detail here, as I'll discuss them in depth in Chapter 3, but the firewall Microsoft supplies is extremely effective.

The advanced firewall offers IT pros and advanced users the ability to control the firewall on a port, app, or service level, ensuring that users can gain access to critical business systems, such as network shares, while maintaining high levels of security.

Many companies and organizations still choose to replace the default Windows firewall with a third-party solution. This is because third-party products can be more flexible, powerful, and more frequently updated than the Microsoft-provided solution.

Malicious Software Removal Tool

The Malicious Software Removal Tool is delivered monthly as part of Windows Update, but you can also download it manually from http://pcs.tv/2c7CUXn, if you suspect you have malware on your PC.

You can think of this tool as an extra, offline antivirus package that will check your PC for the current major malware threats and assist in removing them, if any exist.

I list this as being optional for Windows 7 and Windows 8.1, because it's only with Windows 10 that security and stability updates are mandatory in Windows Update and cannot be disabled.

Windows Update

Speaking of Windows Update, which makes for a nice segue, this is the feature of Windows that keeps the OS up to date with the latest security, stability, and feature updates.

Windows Update should not be disabled on Windows 7 and 8.1 systems, as not having a machine that's fully patched and up to date poses a significant security risk in itself.

You'll no doubt be familiar with Windows Update and know that you can choose when to install updates, hide them, and schedule when updates are downloaded and at what time of the day, if at all, and your PC restarts.

With Windows 10, everything is different. You cannot block, or hide, any security or stability updates for the OS at all. Not even a system administrator has those rights any more. A tool does exist to hide updates on a per-PC basis, and you can download it from http://pcs.tv/2cWj9BP, but this can only be done retrospectively, after an update has already been installed and then removed from the OS.

Two business branches exist in Windows 10 that permit deferment of feature updates, by which Microsoft means new features and upgrades to the OS. The Current Branch for Business (CBB) is available in all installations of Windows 10 Pro (see Figure 2-3). Checking this option will defer feature updates for a period of a few months. In fact, Microsoft doesn't say how long the deferment is for, but the general thinking is that it is around three months.

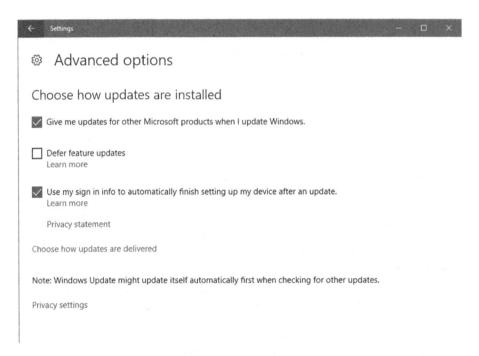

Figure 2-3. *CBB permits deferment of feature updates in Windows 10 Pro*

The other business branch is called *Long Term Servicing Branch (LTSB)*, and this is available only on Windows 10 Enterprise editions. Activating LTSB will defer feature updates for ten years, which Microsoft says is the expected lifetime of an average PC.

As I mentioned earlier, however, neither of these branches will block *any* security or stability updates from being installed in any edition of Windows 10.

Windows Startup Security

In Chapter 1, I discussed the dangers of rootkit infections on PCs and how an Intel-developed technology is mandatory on all PCs sold with Windows 8.1 or later versions. There is, in fact, a series of technologies available in Windows 8.1 and Windows 10 (not Windows 7) that helps guard against boot sector malware.

BitLocker Encryption

It's worth beginning this section by noting that encrypting the hard disk(s) on a PC through use of a security feature such as BitLocker, which is provided with every Pro and Enterprise edition of Windows, can help secure a PC from attack. This is because encrypted drives are kept locked and secure, until the user password is entered at the sign-in screen.

A BitLocker-encrypted PC in which the user is signed out is much more secure from malware, rootkits, and theft than one that is not encrypted.

Secure Boot

First developed by Intel, Secure Boot performs two tasks when a PC is switched on and before the OS loads. First, it verifies that the motherboard firmware is digitally signed, which helps reduce the risk of rootkits, which will modify the firmware and, thus, corrupt the signature.

Secure Boot then queries the digital signature of the OS in the bootloader to see if it matches a cryptographic signature that's stored within the UEFI firmware. If both signatures match, the OS is permitted to load. If they don't, Secure Boot concludes that the bootloader has been tampered with and will prevent the OS from starting.

This isn't always good news, however. I've previously mentioned that Windows 7 does not support Secure Boot, nor can it store its cryptographic signature in the PC's firmware when it's installed. Many Linux distros don't support Secure Boot either, though the most common distros do, and information is available on their web sites. Having Secure Boot enabled means that an OS that doesn't have a valid cryptographic signature will not be permitted to boot.

There are ways around this. Some UEFI systems will allow you to register a bootloader as "safe," while you can also disable Secure Boot on some, but not all, UEFI systems. If you plan to install an OS that does not support UEFI on a new PC, it's worth checking the firmware, or the motherboard manual, before you purchase the PC, to see if Secure Boot can be switched off, or if it will allow you to add non-signed operating systems.

Trusted Boot

Another feature exclusive to Windows 8.1 and Windows 10, Trusted Boot takes over once the OS begins to load. This system checks the OS kernel and all other OS components, such as drivers, start-up files, Early Launch Anti-Malware (more on that in a minute), and all other Windows components, to see if any has been modified.

If it finds that a component *has* been modified, it will refuse to load that component. Windows has an automatic feature that will then run in the background and attempt to repair the damaged or modified component.

Early Launch Anti-Malware

One of the problems with security in legacy versions of Windows was that malware could often load before users' antivirus software, and, thus, it could interfere with that software and prevent detection or removal of itself.

Early Launch Anti-Malware (ELAM) prevents this and also prevents a rootkit from disguising itself as an antivirus driver and loading. ELAM will launch a verified antivirus driver before all other drivers in what Microsoft calls a "chain of trust."

It does this by examining all drivers that start with the OS and determining if they are signed and on a list of trusted drivers. If they're not on the list, they won't be loaded.

All major antivirus packages support ELAM, which is only available in Windows 8.1 and Windows 10. It should be noted, however, that the main antivirus software will load later in the boot process, meaning that while ELAM is a helpful defense, it's not the full antivirus package.

Anti-Malware Features

Another helpful segue, and it's on to the subject of the specific anti-malware features in the Windows OS. As with other features I've already listed, they do tend to vary from one OS version to another, with Windows 7 being the least supported.

Windows SmartScreen

Windows SmartScreen is an online feature of many Microsoft products, including Windows 7 (where it's called the Phishing Filter), Windows 8.1, Windows 10, and some online services as well.

Because the service runs online, it is always kept up to date. It checks incoming e-mails and downloads against white- and blacklists of known phishing sites and malware payloads, and if it finds something that's known to be malicious, it blocks it.

There are a few problems with SmartScreen as it currently stands, however (it is hoped that Microsoft will address these over time). It will occasionally find a download that it's not sure about. The dialog that SmartScreen displays for you advises strongly against executing the download, but the interface is crafted in such a way as to make it difficult to open or run the downloaded file, should you wish to.

The other problem is bigger, as both Internet Explorer 11 (IE11), in all supported versions of Windows, and the Edge browser, along with the Settings app in Windows 8.1 and Windows 10, include a simple switch to turn the feature off (see Figure 2-4). None of these has any proper description of what SmartScreen is or why it's important, and no UAC prompt is required to be clicked to deactivate the feature. Given that all three methods are easy for end users to find and click, I hope this is something Microsoft will address in future builds of Windows 10.

Figure 2-4. *SmartScreen can be too easily disabled by users*

Windows Defender/Security Essentials

Windows Defender is the free/included antivirus package for Windows. It's built into Windows 8.1 and Windows 10 and is activated by default. In Windows 7, it's an optional download that you can get from `http://pcs.tv/2cZ6Ch5`. Additionally, in Windows 7, it's called *Microsoft Security Essentials*, which differentiates it from a separate anti-spyware package in the OS called Windows Defender, which looks and operates in a manner extremely similar to Security Essentials (and indeed Windows Defender) but does a completely different job. I just wanted to make that clear.

I'm not going to make any comments about the effectiveness of Windows Defender as an antivirus package, as the effectiveness of security suites varies from year to year. As a *basic* package, however, it's effective enough, and it has the added bonus of being incredibly lightweight, with almost no negative effect on performance or boot time. Most businesses or organizations, however, and, indeed, the author of this book, will install a third-party anti-virus product.

Windows Defender Offline

Later in this book, I'll detail the offline antivirus tools you can download, from which you can boot your PC to scan for malware, without having to boot into an infected OS, as malware can often prevent security software from running on the desktop.

Windows Defender Offline can be downloaded from `http://pcs.tv/2c8dSlI`, but if you're using Windows 10, you also have the feature built into the OS. Open the Settings app and navigate to Update & security, and then Windows Defender, and you can scroll down the page to see an option to start Windows Defender Offline (see Figure 2-5).

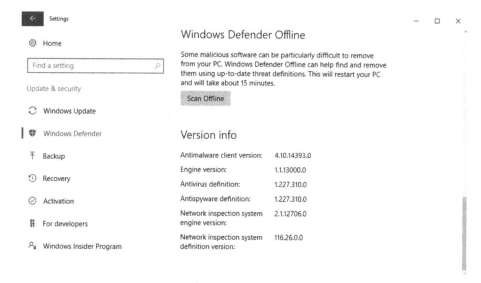

Figure 2-5. *You can launch Windows Defender Offline from the Settings app*

Windows Defender Offline (I'm beginning to feel this should be a drinking game!) will restart the PC and scan for, and attempt to remove, any malware it finds.

Other Security Features

The core security, startup security, and anti-malware features of Windows aren't by any means all of the security features built into the OS. The final one comes with the unassuming name *The Windows Store*.

App Containers

When you install a Win32 traditional desktop program on your PC, it installs into the \Program Files folder from which, with administrative privileges, it can see and access every other file and folder on the machine, including critical Windows operating system files.

Then along came app stores, and with them came containers. Containers are protected areas of storage and memory. Think of them as little virtual machines, each with its own segregated area of memory and storage.

Permissions are assigned to store apps, each of which must be approved by a user. If the user doesn't want the app to be able to access her documents folders, her geolocation or another feature, such as her webcam, the OS will simply block the app from using it.

The Windows Store contains a great many apps that are useful in the workplace, such as the mobile editions of Word, Excel, PowerPoint, and OneNote. Microsoft has included a developer feature, however, that also allow Win32 apps to be containerized and placed in the store.

This includes the full desktop editions of Microsoft Office apps, and it additionally gives those apps to store-only features, such as Sharing tools.

■ **Tip** Running store apps instead of full Win32 desktop apps can boost the battery life of a laptop, ultrabook, or tablet, as these apps are suspended by the OS when they're not in focus. This prevents them from using processor time when you're busy doing something else. Additionally, running an app (any app) full-screen will also boost your battery life, as the graphics processor has fewer things to render.

It's worth noting, too, that if you're using Windows 10 on a low-power ARM-based PC, laptop, ultrabook, tablet, or smartphone, and you're able to install and use Win32 desktop software, this will all be containerized, due to the re-architected nature of the ARM editions of the Windows 10 OS. These apps will also, typically, but not always, come from the Windows Store.

Why is this significant, you ask? While not every software house will place its products in the Windows Store, containerizing any app makes it significantly more resilient against a malware infection and prevents it from being able to interact with the underlying OS in a way that could prove malicious.

32-Bit (×86) and 64-Bit (×64) PCs

It's actually very difficult to find a new PC on sale these days that contains a 32-bit processor (CPU), unless you're buying a budget tablet or laptop. If you're using Windows 7 in a business environment, however, you may still be using and supporting them.

32-bit desktop CPUs, which began with the Intel 386 series in 1985 and ran through to the Pentium 4 chips of 2004, don't support virtualization. This means that, even though Windows 10 comes in a 32-bit variant, older processors and motherboards won't support technologies such as app containers. At `http://pcs.tv/2cXeWeh`, you can check if your Intel processor supports virtualization. At `http://pcs.tv/2cE9aAs`, AMD provides information on virtualization in its processors.

Also, some older 64-bit processors and motherboards don't support hardware virtualization, which means that they won't support all the virtualization features of Windows, which can include app containers. It's always wise to check the documentation that came with your processor and motherboard, when deciding whether to migrate the PC to Windows 10 or if it might be best to retire the unit and purchase a replacement.

While 64-bit installations of Windows are more secure than their 32-bit counterparts, this has more to do with the security features the 64-bit architecture supports and is no guarantee that a system will be secure by default. One of the advantages of 64-bit Windows systems, however, is that hardware and software drivers, which are a common method for malware attack, must be digitally signed by the manufacturer and Microsoft, in order to be supported and loaded at startup.

■ **Note** Microsoft is no longer supporting the latest Intel processors for new installations of Windows 7 and Windows 8.1, and one can assume this also extends to AMD processors as well. This means that there is no driver support available for some processors, and the OS will fail to install. You can check if your PC is compatible with Windows 7 and Windows 8.1 at `http://pcs.tv/2cEciMV`.

Restricting Access to Files

Several times in this book, I've mentioned ransomware and detailed just how disastrous it can be if you find all of your files, or indeed an entire hard disk, encrypted and inaccessible.

The tools I've detailed throughout this chapter focus on protecting the core OS and your apps from malware. Protecting your files, however, requires a bit of thought and perhaps some careful planning.

When you look at the way we manage, store, and back up our files, you'll commonly find that the moment you click Save, the file (or a backup copy of it) is automatically saved to a server store, or a cloud service, such as Office 365, OneDrive, Dropbox, Amazon S3, or Google Drive.

This is brilliant in general use, as it means our files are backed up seamlessly and silently, without us having to do anything about it. We can even use a feature such as File History in Windows 8.1 or Windows 10 to create multiple "versions" of files, which can be restored at a later date, should a change be made to a file accidentally.

Ransomware, however, takes full advantage of our desire to have everything backed up immediately and silently. The moment a file on your hard disk is encrypted, that registers as a file change, and your backup software, be it File History, a cloud sync package, or a third-party backup app—and not being very clever—will automatically back up the new encrypted version of the file.

You may be lucky, in that you'll have version control, meaning that you can take your file storage offline in the event of a ransomware attack, and after cleaning the malware from the PC, restore the earlier version of the file. This, however, relies on your having at least double the amount of backup storage for your files as you use to store the files themselves, and many people and businesses not only won't have this, they won't think of it either.

The solution is to limit ransomware's access to your backups, and there's really only one safe and secure way to do this, even though it's far from foolproof.

This is to have a completely separate backup of your files that runs on a periodic schedule, perhaps every week or every two weeks. This means that if ransomware hits, you will know that you have a backup you can return to that will not have been affected by the encryption.

I say this isn't foolproof because in this circumstance, it's highly likely (Murphy's law being what it is) that the ransomware will strike only a day or perhaps even earlier before your next backup is scheduled to begin.

The problems presented by ransomware mean that we all have to think very carefully about the way we store and back up our files and documents. We must make sure that we all have ample space for file versioning and enough redundancy in the system to ensure that we can recover a copy of our files, even if we lose a week or two's worth, so that we can continue working.

This is, I'm sure, something that backup, cloud, and security vendors will address in the coming years, but it does need to be something you, and your business, plan for today.

Summary

There are many features and facilities built into Microsoft Windows that can help you defend against malware and prevent it from infecting your PC. Migrating your PCs to Windows 10 can help greatly in this regard, as it contains more and better security features than any previous version of the OS. Also, with Windows 10 being the final version of the OS, and with it being regularly updated with new features, the security of the OS will only improve over time.

This is in stark contrast to Windows 7 and Windows 8.1, which now remain feature-locked. Windows 7 is already out of mainstream support, with extended (security and stability) support ending in January 2020. Windows 8.1 mainstream support ends (or ended, depending on when you read this) in January 2018, with extended support ending in January 2023.

There is one security feature, which may confuse you, that I've hardly mentioned in this chapter. This is Windows Firewall. Firewalls are, after all, an essential utility for defending against malware, hacking, and other types of attack. In the next chapter, we'll look at Windows Firewall and Windows Firewall with Advanced Security in depth, along with more detailed ways you can defend your PC from attack.

■ ■ ■

CHAPTER 3

Malware Defense in Depth

Protecting your PC against malware is essential. Often, people ask me what the best antivirus software is. It is not a simple case of buying a malware protection software suite from the retail store. Having only one barrier between you and the hacker, such as a firewall or anti-malware application, could leave you vulnerable to attack. If a software exploit in one of your installed applications is discovered before the vendor can fix the issue and generate a patch, your system could easily be hacked.

Although any method of keeping the bad guys out is thought as being better than none, we recommend that you use multiple layers of protection. This is known as defense in depth and is the practice of layering defenses to provide greater protection. In this chapter, I will discuss some protection mechanisms that you should consider when using Windows.

Firewalls

All modern versions of Windows include a very competent software-based firewall. Firewalls can be software-running as part of an operating system or run on an appliance such as a router, modem, or a dedicated firewall device.

■ **Note**   The Windows Firewall was first introduced in Windows XP, with the second service pack, and is turned on by default when SP2 is installed.

Firewalls examine network traffic that is attempting to make its way across a network interface and onto your computer. Depending on the settings employed, the firewall software can block or allow the traffic and log the successful transmissions and failed attempts. An incorrectly configured firewall, or a computer without a personal firewall, is vulnerable to remote connections being made directly to the local system's services. Only allowed network traffic should gain access to the internal resources classed as being inside your firewall, such as your PC, as shown in Figure 3-1.

© Andrew Bettany and Mike Halsey 2017
A. Bettany and M. Halsey, *Windows Virus and Malware Troubleshooting*,
DOI 10.1007/978-1-4842-2607-0_3

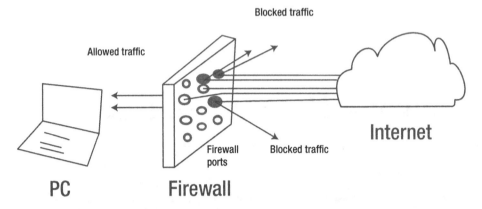

Figure 3-1. *Firewall blocks unwanted traffic*

When a firewall is operational, network packets attempting to gain access to your computer will believe that your computer does not exist, as the firewall does not respond, and the hacker will in all likelihood move to the next computer and attempt to gain access there.

A common statement I hear is that "I won't get hacked/attacked; we are too small to be of interest to a hacker." This sounds plausible, especially when you consider that there are billions of devices connected to the Internet; however, it is not entirely true in practice. The hacker will direct his or her efforts based on the following criteria:

1. Ease of access

2. Likely return (typically financial)

3. Risk of being caught

4. Challenge

If you have little protection, you fall into the first category, and this determination is generally fully exploited by the automated use of an investigative bot (short for *robot*). Bots are able to analyze tens of thousands of computers that are connected to the Internet every minute. Because Windows computers will generally try to respond to other computers (that is how they communicate), if your computer acknowledges its own presence in response to a Ping request or other query from a bot, it will immediately be escalated to the next level of interest for the hacker/malware software to investigate.

We regularly see reports of laptops being hacked when using public Wi-Fi in areas such as cafés, fast food restaurants, and airports. Although the majority of popular social media sites now require HTTPS connections, which are secured using the Secure Sockets Layer (SSL), these high-level protection mechanisms can be bypassed easily if the firewall has been disabled or if file and printer sharing has been enabled for public networks.

By default, if you are running Windows Vista or later versions, your PC is protected from other computers seeing your PC on the network. However, if these settings have been modified within the Network and Sharing Center, to allow network discovery and file and printer sharing on shared or public networks, as shown in Figure 3-2, your PC could be easily comprised.

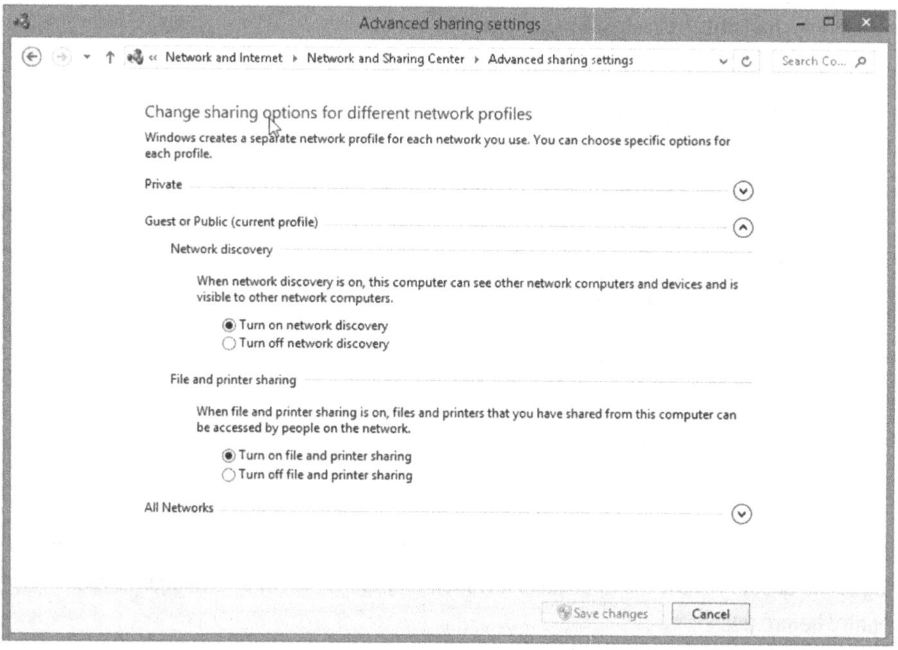

Figure 3-2. *Modifying advanced sharing settings*

Understanding that it is essential that you have some barrier against attack is paramount in keeping safe, and the firewall is often the easiest protection to enable.

Keylogging Software

Individuals and home users are very attractive to hackers. This is because average users are unaware beyond the very basics of protecting their PCs. A home user will trust her PC with sensitive private information, such as banking and social media access. She will protect her login password but may freely provide Wi-Fi or printer access to a guest. If a hacker can gain access to the PC, it is very easy for him to install malware or other monitoring tools, such as a keylogger, which can relay all keystrokes, web page screenshots, and other PC activity directly back to the potential thief. Even a guest could inadvertently install a virus or keylogger simply by using an infected USB drive on your PC.

Keylogger software monitors the activity of a computer, such as keeping track of which programs are run or closed, all web sites visited, and any keystrokes used, including passwords. Some keyloggers will also record screenshots of all activity and

23

either store the content logs locally or upload them discretely to a remote store that the hacker can harvest.

Some common keylogger features include the following:

- Captures all keystrokes

- Records instant messages

- Invisible in Task Manager

- Support for dual monitors

- Auto uninstall at a specific date

If you want to understand the impressive level of detail that a keylogger can obtain from a PC, review the features of some sample keyloggers in Table 3-1.

Table 3-1. Keylogging Software

Keylogger	Web Site
Actual Keylogger	www.actualkeylogger.com/
Best Free Keylogger	bestxsoftware.com/
Keystroke Spy	www.spytech-web.com

■ **Note** Installing a keylogger onto a PC for which you do not have permission may be illegal. You should review the applicable laws relating to the use of a keylogger in your country before use.

Software Firewalls

Personal (or host-based) firewalls refer to a software firewall that is either integrated into Windows or installed as a separate application designed to protect a single endpoint, such as a laptop or PC.

Although a personal firewall only protects the single device, it still performs a useful function inside the network, as it prevents or slows down anyone trying to directly access the PC over the network.

Examples of vendors who offer software-based firewalls that either complement or replace the Windows built-in firewall are shown in Table 3-2. Most consumers and small businesses will purchase a software firewall for a one-off fee that includes the first year of updates and is then chargeable as an annual subscription for ongoing virus signature updates.

Table 3-2. *Personal Firewall Software*

Firewall	Vendor	Web Site
Norton Internet Security	Symantec	`norton.com/internet-security`
Internet Security	Trend Micro	`www.trendmicro.com/`
McAfee Total Protection	McAfee	`www.mcafee.com`
Sophos Home	Sophos	`www.sophos.com/lp/sophos-home.aspx`

Most Internet security software now offers a comprehensive suite of tools that includes additional features in addition to firewall protection, such as

- Anti-ransomware, spyware, antivirus, and anti-malware

- Phishing and identity theft protection

- Dangerous web sites blocking

- Secure online storage

- Support for multiple devices

Organizational Firewalls

Within an organization, a dedicated hardware firewall is generally used to safeguard incoming network traffic that is connecting from the Internet. This is useful to protect company-owned public facing IP addresses that may be used for services such as FTP, Intranet, SharePoint, and web sites.

With a hardware appliance, you simply plug the device into your network topology, and you're ready to configure firewall rules that restrict, allow, or redirect network traffic, based on your requirements.

In this book, I can't recommend specific manufacturers of hardware-based firewalls, although some of the well-known brands include Barracuda, Cisco, SonicWALL, and WatchGuard.

In nearly all scenarios, firewall appliances are more expensive than software-based firewalls. The cost of the appliance generally increases with the capacity and features. When choosing, you should ensure the device is well-suited to your needs, by considering the following factors:

- *Brand awareness and reputation*

- *Capacity* : The device has to manage the load, speed, and number of network nodes being actively managed.

- *Failover capability*: If the device fails, or becomes swamped during an attack, how does it respond? Will it failover to another appliance, allow or block all connections?

- *Technical support*: Because the device is a crucial component of your network, you must ensure that help is on hand when you need it. Ideally, there should be solid support-forum technical help available.

- *Budget*: Most buying decisions often boil down to price. Ensure that you purchase a device that will perform as required, then look for budget alignment.

Blacklists and Whitelists

To reduce the likelihood of self-harm from internal users, many organizations monitor and restrict access by staff to specific external locations.

If the threat of attack or risk to the business is sufficiently high, the firewall can be used to actively block outbound traffic to known malware sites or known access points, such as peer-to-peer file sharing sites or Dark Web gateway portals.

■ **Note** The Dark Web, or Dark Net, is a special part of the Internet that is encrypted and allows users to anonymize their actions. It has, therefore, become a network on which black market illegal activities take place.

You could also employ techniques, such as blocking IP addresses, using blacklists. These lists contain domains and IP addresses of known and potential malicious attack sources. It is possible to automate the regular updating of firewall blacklists by using tools such as Fail2ban (`www.fail2ban.org/`), which automatically maintains your blacklists, based on malicious behavior.

By using a blacklist, your firewall can be highly effective at restricting outbound traffic, and a modern firewall will have negligible impact on the appliance performance, even with blacklists containing tens of thousands of entries.

Firewalls can monitor inbound activity and automatically block or ignore any IP traffic, if it is exhibiting potential malicious behavior, such as probing or "door rattling." For specific scenarios, such as on the research and development network, a firewall can even be configured to block all ingress.

Have you ever noticed that when you have a potential customer who is accessing your web site often, perhaps you have a discounted sale in place? You may experience many page views from the same external source. To prevent inadvertently blocking potential customers from your customer facing web sites, when short-term excessive activity occurs, it can be more appropriate to temporarily block access to suspicious IP addresses, as this often is a sufficient deterrent. You have to carefully set the threshold metric for when you trigger these blocks. This could be initially set at 100 attempts and then reviewed.

Remember that most firewall attacks are bot-generated, and, generally, when a bot finds a firewall that is not vulnerable, it will move to target the next IP address in its line of attack. Where a bot finds a firewall or ports that are expressly open, the "finder" bot will flag these IPs as "live" for another bot to perform deeper penetration testing. These scan results are often available to purchase on the Dark Web.

The Rise of the Internet of Things

We are currently at the dawn of a new era in computing—the rise of the Internet of Things (IoT). You can currently buy Internet-connected TVs, alarm clocks, radios, and even refrigerators that can reorder groceries automatically when they run low.

With IoT, devices located within your home can communicate directly to servers on the Internet. This is made possible by using your home Wi-Fi network, which creates an IPv6 bridge between the interface that serves the IoT device directly to your Internet service provider. In this way, for example, your Internet-connected popcorn maker can be turned on just as you leave the office, so that you have piping hot popcorn for the evening movie.

Interface-, port-, and application-level IP forwarding allows your single public IP address provided by your ISP to allow access to multiple devices behind your firewall, often without your knowledge.

You should certainly be vigilant and aware of the potential risks with IoT, especially as they are an emerging technology for which standardized security procedures and precautions have not yet been formalized.

Consider the implications arising if, after installing a new IoT-based security CCTV camera system onto your home or business network, hackers were able to access the data feed?

The Windows Advanced Firewall

Windows comes with two different firewall interfaces: the default Windows Firewall and the Windows Firewall with Advanced Security.

Many users will never step beyond the functionality offered by the Windows Firewall, shown in Figure 3-3.

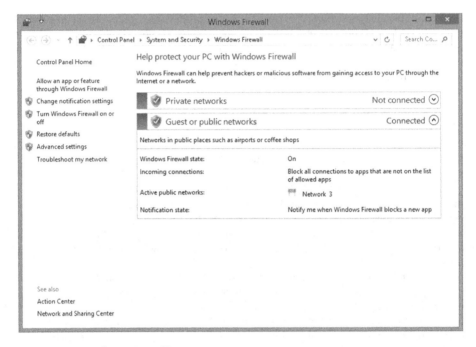

Figure 3-3. *Windows Firewall*

In Windows XP, the initial Windows Firewall drew a lot of criticism for its limitations. Windows Firewall was unidirectional and would not stop outbound connections to the Internet, and it would not filter IPv6 traffic. If the user used an administrator account (as many users did with XP), viruses could easily disable the firewall, and this further weakened the reputation of the built-in protection.

Thankfully, Microsoft upgraded the firewall quickly and enabled Automatic Updates and the Windows Security Center, which addressed many of the earlier failings.

For those users with administrative abilities who have to configure advanced settings, such as fine-tuning a VPN connection or monitoring firewall logs, you must click the Advanced Settings link, as shown in Figure 3-4, or type "wf.msc" into the Run or Search command.

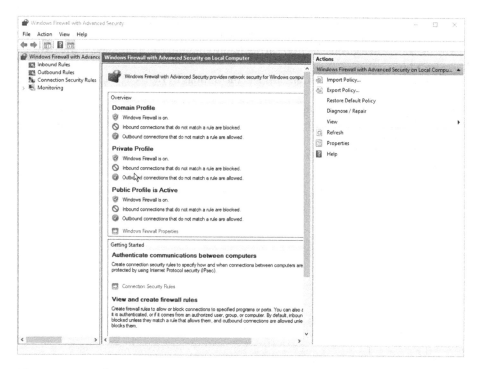

Figure 3-4. *Windows Firewall with Advanced Security*

The Windows Firewall with Advanced Security management console was introduced with Windows Vista and provides access to many advanced options and enables remote administration.

From the console, you can configure the following:

- *Inbound Rules*: Traditional firewall capability to prevent network ingress.

- *Outbound Rules*: Blocks outbound traffic, such as preventing malware that attempts to "phone home"

- *Connection Security Rules*: Used to set up advanced VPN and tunneling and set configuration settings

- *Monitoring*: Used to log inbound and outbound traffic through the firewall

Windows Firewall with Advanced Security allows a great deal of low-level packet filtering and refining of network traffic, such as the ability to filter source and destination IP addresses and port ranges and data type, such as UDP or TCP.

To create a new inbound rule, launch the Windows Firewall with Advanced Security management console and click New Rule in the Action pane on the right-hand side.

Follow the New Inbound Rule Wizard, to create your rule, and once complete, the new rule will appear in the list of Inbound Rules in the center pane. If the rule is active, it will be marked with a green check box in the Name column, and if disabled, it will have a gray check box.

You can and review any rule and inspect the settings by right-clicking a rule and selecting Properties.

In the Properties window, the selected rule settings are displayed in a tabbed format. You can edit the rule and change any of the available parameters, as shown in Figure 3-5.

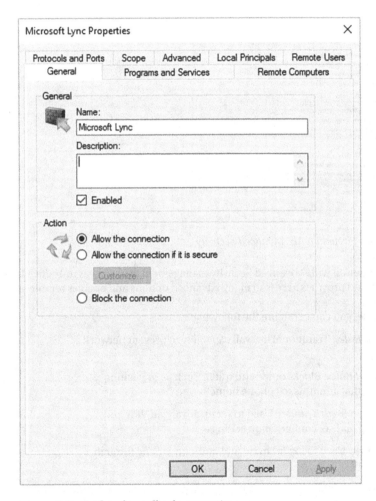

Figure 3-5. *Explore firewall rule properties*

If you scroll through the inbound and outbound rules, you will see that there are many rules built into Windows.

Connection security rules allow you to implement very secure traffic between endpoints, such as between remote computers or between specific IP addresses across the network or Internet.

As an example, you may require that only encrypted network traffic is permitted for all communications to a secure payment gateway server on your internal network. This could be achieved by creating a connection security rule within Windows Firewall with Advanced Security, which uses the server-to-server rule and forces connections to be allowed only if connections use IPsec security certificates.

IPsec is often used to secure server-to-server traffic within high-security environments. Hacking into the network stream and decrypting the packet contents protected by IPsec is not possible unless the certificates or pre-shared keys (PSK) have already been compromised.

■ **Note** Following the recent disclosures by Edward Snowden relating to network attacks, it is recommended that all routers have their firmware upgraded to the latest version and to maintain strong pre-shared keys or use certificates.

Connection security rules are often used in corporate environments and are set by the network administrator. You should take care if you configure them to ensure that you do not inadvertently lock yourself out of a network or prevent connections when you enable a new rule.

In addition to the GUI tools with the Control Panel, you can also configure firewall settings via the command prompt, PowerShell, and by using Group Policy, as shown in Figure 3-6.

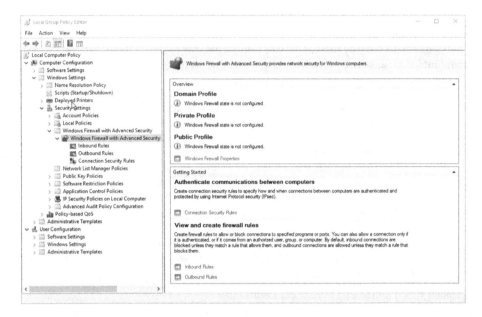

Figure 3-6. *Configure firewall settings using Group Policy*

The firewall settings within Group Policy can be found with the following node: Computer Configuration ➤ Windows Settings ➤ Security Settings ➤ Windows Firewall with Advanced Security.

Demilitarized Zone

Demilitarized zone (DMZ) is a term that is often used when discussing networking, but it can be quite complicated to define in a concise manner. DMZ refers to a network zone that you control that is used to separate the untrusted Internet from your internal (trusted) network.

If you think of your network as an inner circle of trust, the DMZ is an outer ring, and, finally, the internet is the outermost ring around that, as shown in Figure 3-7. The rings of defense are similar to the defense-in-depth concept mentioned at the beginning of this chapter.

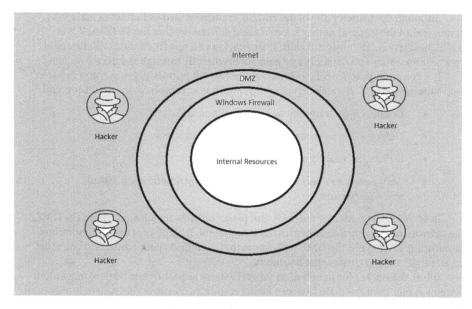

Figure 3-7. *DMZ used to protect internal resources*

The inner circle is protected by the operating system, then the firewall, then, finally, the DMZ. For each ring, there is an internal- and external-facing network interface. In a high-volume environment, separate physical devices are used to separate different types of traffic and direction of flow.

Typically, a business will use hardware-based firewall appliances for the DMZ, as these tend to be more resilient against attack. Additionally, being built on a Linux subsystem, they are often more robust and hardened, due to their small footprint.

To harden the perimeter and make the DMZ security more secure, each firewall appliance can be restricted to allow only specific protocols, as required by the organization. These could include

- *File Transfer Protocol (FTP)*: TCP ports 20, 21

- *DNS*: TCP port 53, UDP port 53

- *Simple Mail Transport Protocol (SMTP)*: TCP port 25

- *Hypertext Transfer Protocol (HTTP)*: TCP port 80

- *HTTPS*: TCP port 443

- *System management often uses SSH*: TCP port 22

It is recommended that unnecessary or end-user protocols, such as NETBIOS, which could be used to navigate with the DMZ and locate vulnerabilities inside the DMZ, be disabled.

Although the primary role of the DMZ is to prevent further ingress of malicious action within the internal network, you should still ensure that the DMZ itself is at the highest level of defense and alert. If an attacker can penetrate the DMZ, he could compromise other DMZ routers and gain access directly through to internal systems.

It is common practice for a business to locate web portals, gateways, and extranet web sites in the DMZ. If a web server in the DMZ is compromised, the attacker could

- Delete, copy, or modify web applications and data

- Deface external company web sites and extranets

- Deface internal company intranet sites

- Gain access to internal resources, including databases, backups, and source code

In addition to restricting the ports and protocols that are allowed within the DMZ, the network or security manager must ensure that the DMZ is kept under continuous monitoring. Effectively, the DMZ is the moat that surrounds your castle, and you must ensure that nothing crosses that boundary.

Often, the hacker (or penetration expert) will try to probe your DMZ management systems rather than the main Internet-facing resources. Because this system is only used infrequently, consider requiring a higher level of protection, such as enabling encryption, authentication, and detailed transaction logging, as well as disabling all access when not in use.

Some useful best practices that can be deployed in relation to the DMZ include the following:

- Use an intrusion prevention system (IPS).

- Implement and deploy a robust security policy.

- Implement a thorough auditing policy.

- Use signatures to detect and block well-known attacks.

- Keep anti-malware signatures up to date.

- Be vigilant.

- Power off maintenance equipment when not in use.

On a regular basis, for example, every six months, and especially if your career and business relies on maintaining a robust and secure DMZ, you should consider hiring the services of a penetration expert.

Under a strict set of rules and boundaries agreed to by you and management, the expert will attempt to hack your system from the outside. The results of the actions will often show where improvements can be made, and they should be safeguarded, as they could contain any deficiencies in your current approach. You should implement countermeasures and remove some or all the vulnerabilities highlighted, at your earliest opportunity.

User Account Control

User Account Control (UAC) has been one of the key security features in Windows since its introduction in Windows Vista. Despite many urban myths, you should not turn off UAC, as it does an excellent job at protecting the whole of Windows.

Despite initial angst from users when it was first introduced, the UAC feature has been improved and gradually refined to be more usable and less intrusive in each version of Windows since Vista.

Windows 10 strengthens the security further by displaying the computer background image as the secure desktop whenever the UAC prompt is required, as shown in Figure 3-8. Previous versions of Windows would freeze the background, which prompted the UAC, which could then provide the hacker with the opportunity to hijack.

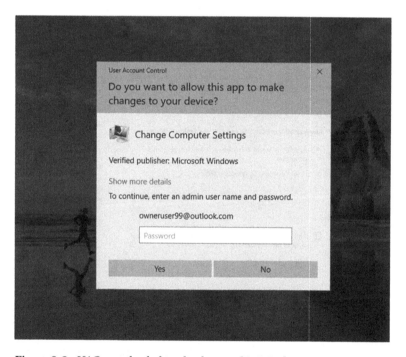

Figure 3-8. *UAC uses the desktop background in Windows 10*

Another useful feature of UAC in Windows 10 is that the UAC prompt will auto exit if no password is entered into the dialog box within 30 seconds.

Prior to UAC, most security breaches were caused by the user unintentionally installing malware, viruses, and unsafe software installation with administrator privileges. For the home user, this is still the case, because home users typically are granted the administrator account privileges that are assigned to the first user account after setup. The problem with the local administrator account is that the user is able to make system-wide changes and is allowed to launch system tools and utilities that can make irreversible changes to Windows.

In Windows 10, the UAC has adopted a new, more colorful set of pop-up messages, and this attempts to make the messaging clearer for the user.

In previous versions of Windows, UAC is largely ignored by the home user, which is primarily due to a lack of awareness of what UAC actually does.

UAC is a key security component against the constant and ever-changing threat from malware and contributes to the defense-in-depth strategy for Windows.

Within an enterprise, UAC is usually strictly enforced and will only appear when a user (or malware) attempts to configure, install software, or modify his system in a way that is not allowed. Thankfully, in the workplace, users seldom try to modify their systems, and where they must install new software, this is requested through the helpdesk.

An administrator can modify the UAC settings, as shown in Figure 3-9, by typing UAC into the Search Windows box and pressing Enter or selecting Change User Account Control settings.

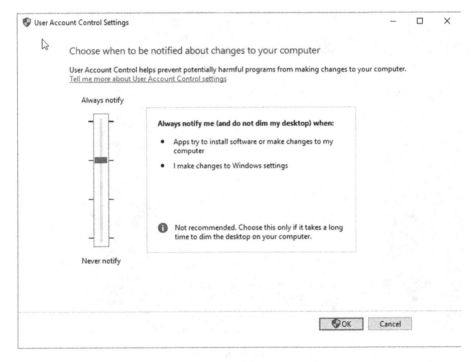

Figure 3-9. Adjusting the UAC settings on Windows 10

Often, users complain that they see the UAC too often, and on a new PC, this may be the case, but once the initial applications and settings have been configured, there should be minimal prompts going forward. A user with a standard user account can perform the following tasks:

- Burn CD/DVD media

- Change the desktop background

- Change the time zone

- Change his/her own user account password

- Configure accessibility options

- Configure power options

- Connect to a Wi-Fi or LAN connection

- Install drivers, either from Windows Update or those that are supplied with Windows

- Install updates from Windows Update

- Modify his/her display settings

- Pair and configure a Bluetooth device with the PC

- Perform other troubleshooting and network diagnostic and repair tasks

- Play CD/DVD media

- Restore own files from File History

- Use Remote Desktop to connect to another PC

- View most settings, although they will require elevated permissions when attempting to change Windows settings

You should be careful of who has administrative accounts, as these users have a great amount of power—they can read, write, execute, and modify all resources and Windows permissions on a PC.

Even as an administrator, Windows will still use the UAC prompt to make you aware that your intended action will perform a task that will have system-wide impact. Although, as an administrator, you will not have to provide your credentials, you do have to provide consent. This is known as Admin Approval Mode.

There are two types of elevation prompts in Windows:

> *Consent*: Only shown to administrators in Admin Approval Mode when they try to perform an administrative task

> *Credential*: Shown to standard users when they attempt to perform an administrative task

Some of the typical scenarios in which a standard user would be prompted by UAC for the elevation to administrative privileges include the following:

- Add or remove a user account

- Browse to another user's directory

- Change user account types

- Change Windows Firewall settings

- Configure Automatic Updates

- Configure Parental Controls

- Install a driver for a device

- Install ActiveX controls

- Install and uninstall applications

- Modify UAC settings

- Move or copy files into the Program Files or Windows directories

- Restore system backup files

- Schedule Automated Tasks

It is not possible to turn off UAC completely, but it is possible to silence the notifications by moving the slider shown in Figure 3-9 all the way down to the bottom (Never Notify).

For administrators who want to configure UAC using Group Policy, there are ten Group Policy settings available in Windows 10, as shown in Figure 3-10. These policy settings are located in the Security Options node found within Security Settings ➤ Local Policies ➤ Security Options.

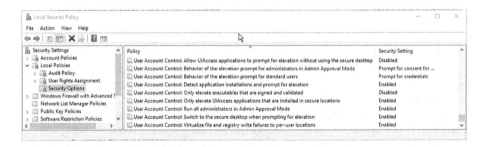

Figure 3-10. *UAC Group Policy settings*

Policy can be set at the local user level, using the Local Security Policy snap-in, or across multiple users in a domain environment, using the Group Policy Management Console.

■ **Note**   A detailed description of all Group Policy settings relating to UAC is provided on TechNet at the following URL: https://technet.microsoft.com/en-gb/itpro/windows/keep-secure/user-account-control-overview.

Summary

In the past, Microsoft Windows has suffered from the clear danger that malware presents to users. We have seen that you may mitigate attacks by employing a defense-in-depth approach. Most threats are time-bound, and if you present a robust or layered set of defenses around your PC, a hacker will, in most cases, abandon his attempt and move to a less defended target. Sometimes, merely stalling or delaying an attack can be a useful strategy.

I have discussed how firewalls can be used to lock down access to unwanted network traffic and can isolate public-facing resources within a DMZ. Firewalls can provide additional protection to our system, while allowing us to provide essential services. UAC is sometimes seen as a hindrance to users, but the persistent inclusion within Windows, and the continued refinement of this tool, is paying security dividends, especially against malware and adventurous employees.

In the next chapter, you will see how malware attacks PCs and networks, how users are targeted, and how you can minimize the risk of attack and infection.

CHAPTER 4

■ ■ ■

Identifying Attacks

Malware will not go away, and it is actually likely to increase, just like it has year after year for the last ten years. Whether it is the slow running of a computer, or a call to the helpdesk reporting a strange message being displayed, users will continue to suffer malware attacks on their PCs, smartphones, and tablets.

In this chapter, I will explore how malware infects PCs and networks, their specific entry points, and payloads. I will discuss how you can protect against infection and minimize the impact of a malware attack.

You will have to understand the symptoms and likely effects of malware, so that you can troubleshoot and identify when a device has been targeted.

How Malware Infects PCs

It is well known that compared to other computing devices, PCs are attacked the most. This is because PCs, and Windows PCs in particular, are generally open systems that have many vulnerabilities. There are several reasons why Windows PCs have become appealing for viruses, these include

- Maintenance of backwards software compatibility

- Home users with administrative privileges

- Open networking stack

- Volume of user base

Apart from the positive effect following the introduction of User Account Control (UAC), mentioned in Chapter 3, it is unlikely that malware infection rates will decrease for Windows PCs going forward.

The symptoms that result from a virus infection can include any or a combination of the following:

- Computer performs tasks very slowly

- Unexplained disk and network activity

- Files don't open with the default application

- Custom pop-up messages, or background images, appear

© Andrew Bettany and Mike Halsey 2017
A. Bettany and M. Halsey, *Windows Virus and Malware Troubleshooting*,
DOI 10.1007/978-1-4842-2607-0_4

- Unexpected command prompt window opens then closes

- PC crashes or hangs or will not boot

- Strange computer behavior

- Too many pop-up windows

- Internet access is very slow compared to normal

Let's consider how malware can infect Windows PCs, then we will consider how you can identify attacks once they have taken place.

There are generally three types of viruses that can infect your PC. These are file-infector viruses, boot sector viruses, and macro viruses, as listed in Table 4-1.

Table 4-1. *Common Types of Viruses*

Virus Type	File Infector	Rootkits and Boot Sector	Macro
Entry mechanism	Within application files	Install in a hard drive's boot sector	Burrow into Microsoft Word and Excel documents
File type	`.EXE` files	Boot sector memory	`.DOCM` or `.XLSM`
Payload	Memory or executable files infection	Copy/infect/delete files	Infected Office templates
Effectiveness	Very effective	Very effective	Generally, affects Office files
Detectability	Virus signature may be known, file size has been changed	Difficult if loaded before Windows. USB/HDD can be detected using signature based virus scanner.	Office blocks macros by default. User must approve each virus.
Removability	Find, delete, and replace original file, usual in Safe Mode	Not easy. Rootkits can prevent the remover software from loading.	Virus scanners can quarantine infected files.

Infector-Type Viruses

Some users may have experienced file-infector type viruses, either directly through an attack or by attending computer security training. This type of attack is the most common and has been around for many years. Because infector-type viruses attach themselves to, or bury inside, another file, they are often detected by a routine antivirus scanner, which can locate the virus, owing to its known virus signature.

A virus signature is a known, characteristic pattern that a virus scanner detects when a virus has been hidden embedded within a program file. Although new viruses are created on a regular basis, antivirus software knows what to look for and has to be updated regularly to keep abreast of the most recent virus signatures.

If a virus is not detected, it can infect system memory and executable files and reside on the device for months and even years.

One classic (and particularly nasty) virus from a few years ago infected systems and behaved as a rogue security program that attempts to scare, threaten, cajole, hector, harangue, pester, aggravate, intimidate, badger, harass, and generally nag the user into paying the hacker to clean his or her system by using the fake security software. The virus, called "Win32/FakeScanti" presented the user with various warnings and a credible-looking security tool named Windows Antivirus Pro, as shown in Figure 4-1.

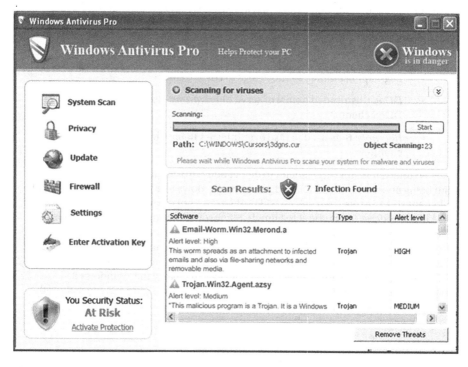

Figure 4-1. *Win32/FakeScanti virus screenshot*

The virus would try to convince users that their systems were unreliable and infected, by periodically rebooting the system and preventing other executables from running, by associating the .exe extension with desot.exe, one of the files installed by Win32/FakeScanti.

Whenever the user tried to run an application, such as an antivirus tool, or even Microsoft Paint, the file name was passed to desot.exe, which then decided to run the application or display a message box with a virus warning.

Thankfully, the Malicious Software Removal Tool (MSRT), which I will discuss in Chapter 5, successfully removes the Win32/FakeScanti virus and its variants.

Rootkits and Boot Sector Viruses

A boot sector virus normally resides in the special area of a hard drive, USB, CD, or DVD and aims to infect a system before Windows or any antivirus software can detect its presence.

Any boot virus that can load and hide inside areas of system memory can potentially remain undetected by Windows indefinitely. You saw in the first two chapters how rootkits and boot sector viruses have become very effective at bypassing traditional anti-malware software detection. They are very sophisticated in their design and execution and are designed to evade detection. Typical payloads of rootkits include

- *Backdoor programs:* Log in backdoors, keyloggers

- *Packet sniffers*: Inspect network traffic from within the network

- *Log-wiping utilities*: Remove logs to cover tracks

- *DDoS* (distributed denial of service) *programs*: Use the PC as a DDoS client

- *IRC/bots*: Bots used to take over Internet Relay Chat (IRC) channels

Even today, it is still very difficult to detect boot viruses, and if you are concerned about being attacked by a rootkit, and you have Windows 8 or Windows 10, you should implement UEFI Secure Boot, which will protect the boot environment.

When Windows 8 was about to launch, Microsoft announced that it would enable UEFI Secure Boot on all new devices using Windows 8 and later versions. Following a massive outcry from concerned users (who believed that Secure Boot would prevent them from dual booting or installing a different operating system), Microsoft backed down and modified its plans a little. All new devices that carry the "Windows 8 Compatible" or "Windows 10 Compatible" logo, as shown in Figure 4-2, must allow the user to turn the Secure Boot feature off.

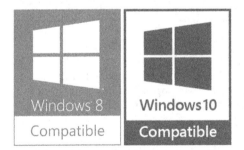

Figure 4-2. Windows compatible logos

■ **Note** If you want to learn more about the Microsoft implementation of Secure Boot, please review the overview found on TechNet, `https://technet.microsoft.com/en-us/library/hh824987.aspx?f=255&MSPPError=-2147217396`.

Modern Linux distributions such as Ubuntu, Fedora, Red Hat Enterprise Linux, and openSUSE currently support Secure Boot and will work without any tweaks on modern hardware, because their boot loader now contains a signed certificate that is recognized by Secure Boot.

It can be difficult to completely remove a rootkit infection. I will introduce some approaches in Chapter 6, but my preferred remedy is to format the drive, flash the UEFI or BIOS, and completely reinstall the operating system. As Lt. Ellen Ripley said in the 1986 movie *Aliens*, "I say we take off and nuke the entire site from orbit. It's the only way to be sure."

Macro Viruses

Originally, macros were used in Microsoft Excel and Word to speed up repetitive tasks. As the technology advanced, macros could be written that not only worked within Microsoft Office applications but could interact fully with the operating system also.

In modern versions of macro viruses, programmable code, such as Visual Basic for Applications (VBA), JavaScript, and .Net, is used that provides the application user and hacker much more creativity.

As macro viruses became more popular, Microsoft began to warn users that macros could be dangerous, and the dialog box displaying "This document contains macros" would alert them to the presence of a macro.

You may wonder why we need a warning about a macro contained within a spreadsheet. Most macros initialize themselves when the spreadsheet or document is opened; therefore, opening a spreadsheet containing a destructive macro virus would potentially create havoc on your machine.

If you received an e-mail from a colleague containing a macro enabled spreadsheet, it would have the file extension .XLSM. This would indicate the e-mail contains an Excel Macro-Enabled Workbook file created in Excel 2007 or newer versions.

If you are not aware that a file contains a macro, you should be cautious and not trust the macro. The file will still open, without the macro being run, and the contents, therefore, will be safe.

After the year 2000, macro viruses began to decline, but in recent years, macro viruses have made a comeback. One cunning tactic employed is for a macro virus to wait for you to open an infected document, and then it will quietly spread into your Office template files. Once your template files are infected, the virus can easily hijack Office every time you use it and infect all the documents that you edit or create thereafter.

Microsoft continues to protect users from macro malware, by restricting macro enabled documents. By using social engineering methods, malware authors are often able to trick susceptible users into enabling macros, thereby bypassing the built-in protection within Office.

E-mail and the Internet

Often e-mail and the Web are blamed for being the source of the majority of malware. This is only partly correct. E-mail and the Internet are now the modern delivery mechanism of malware, but in themselves, they are just the carrier. The malware is still an infected file or a macro that needs to be activated in some way by the user.

Most users have learned not to open suspicious-looking e-mail attachments, and rarely will a proficient user fall prey to a suspicious e-mail payload.

Recently, though, malware writers have become more professional, and e-mails are now better worded, and unless the user is kept up to date with current malware approaches, he or she is more susceptible to a rogue attachment. E-mail scams, together with their attachments, now present themselves as being from a reputable source, bundled with a very credible narrative and goal.

One recent example of how a competent user can fall foul of a modern attack is by relying on a belief that a PDF file is safe. Take the example of a user being sent a delivery note, addressed to her company, and the attachment is a PDF file. Typically, PDF documents are static with safe content. Today, PDF documents can contain rich formatting and dynamic elements, such as JavaScript or XML.

For example, a PDF file can be made to execute an embedded executable file without exploiting any vulnerability, although a warning message is displayed (although it is possible to customize the warning message and, therefore, socially engineer it to persuade the user to accept the warning).

■ **Note**   If you want to review how malicious PDF files can contain viruses, look at the Troj/PDFEx-DF. Sophos discusses it at URL `https://nakedsecurity.sophos.com/2010/04/12/ trojpdfexdf-sophoslabs-sees-malware-exploiting-launch/`.

A company will employ many layers of defense against malware, both internally on PCs and externally on mail servers. In all examples of e-mail borne viruses, it must be remembered that only when someone opens it can the virus activate itself. Vigilance and training of the user must always be the last line of defense.

The human factor can only at best be mitigated. Even with the best security awareness-training program, at least one in a thousand people will still click that well-crafted phishing e-mail.

How Malware Infects Networks

The majority of PCs using the Web now have some form of protection, yet more than 50% will have been infected with malware during the last 12 months.

We have to ascertain how more than half of all PCs can be infected, despite having some protection in place. We can identify potential areas that require urgent attention, including the following:

> *Antivirus software is not operational*: Users often turn off antivirus software because it might negatively affect the performance of their device.

> *Antivirus software is not up to date*: Users believe that their antivirus software is effective once installed. Often, a user is unaware that it requires daily updates, provided by the security vendor.

> *Constant game of cat and mouse*: Anti-malware software needs to keep track of hundreds, or even thousands, of signatures related to possible viruses. This is updated daily and requires 100% proficiency by the security vendor.

> *Old applications are vulnerable*: Older versions of applications, plug-ins, and operating systems beyond their end of life (EOL) can be exploited by malware.

> *Anti-malware software incorrectly configured*: Security software designed to protect against malware is increasingly difficult for the average user to configure and set up on-demand scans, scheduled scans, e-mail scans, download scans, and on-use scans.

> *Ineffective anti-malware software*: Not all anti-malware is as effective as others. The rise of freeware anti-malware software makes the choice extremely difficult for the user.

> *Multiple installations of anti-malware software*: Not all anti-malware software will detect specialist attacks, such as spyware or adware infections, so users are forced to install two of more security solutions. Unfortunately, rival security products often fail to work nicely with each other, which can leave gaps for malware to slip through.

When deployed, most PCs typically will be performing their ability to detect and deter malware well. Often, users adopt a "set and forget" approach to security and will seldom check to see if their anti-malware solution continues to work, or if their PC is being routinely updated.

We have seen how, through poorly configured or maintained devices, malware can slip through the barrier created by traditional antivirus systems.

Malware can attack the network itself and the PC. An attack can aim for several possible outcomes, some of these are

- Exfiltration theft of data

- Identity, intellectual property theft

- Data corruption/deletion

- Disruption of operations, reputation

- Payment of ransom, profit motive

If we analyze some of the most common types of attacks, as shown in Table 4-2, we can detect their motives.

Table 4-2. *Common Malware Attack Vectors and Motives*

Motive	DDoS attack	Virus	Phishing	Ransomware	Trojan Horse
Exfiltration / theft of data		x			x
Profit		x	x	x	x
Data corruption / deletion		x			
Disruption of operations / take over	x	x			x
Identity theft		x	x		x
Awareness / spotlight	x				

It is clear to see that the motivation for creating malware has shifted from fame and notoriety to profit.

Malware authors now direct their efforts to bypass client-based security and operate in stealth mode, concealing itself within the operating system, using rootkit technology, whereby it can then disable any existing anti-malware software and take control of network access. Once the malware is in place, it can then steal data and user identities, until detected.

If malware can gain access to a PC via the Web, it has the potential to connect to other devices, using Windows networking.

Access to the network will often be a key objective for most malware, because access to the network is likely to deliver some beneficial goal. Malware uses the network to (1) provide a backdoor on the system, (2) spread viruses to other machines, or (3) contact the virus authors and allow remote control of a PC or server.

Ever since the early versions of Windows, Microsoft has employed a very open approach to file sharing and networking. Left unchecked, it can offer areas for malware to attempt exploits such as

- *Access shared files across the network using the Server Message Block (SMB) protocol*: Upgrade to latest SMB version.

- *Access via network-connected multifunction printers and copier*: Monitor and use complex passwords.

- *Available administrative shares, such as C\$, IPC\$, and ADMIN\$:* Remove them if they are not required.

- *Internal web-server vulnerability (they should be as secure as your DMZ web-servers)*

Network administrators should employ NTFS and password-protected file sharing and ensure that no resources are left accessible, unless by an authenticated user.

Thankfully, Windows networking is a great deal more secure since the release of Windows Vista. With Vista, Microsoft fully redesigned the implementation of the TCP/IP stack to allow for an IPv4/IPv6 dual stack. It also engineered several performance enhancements (Jumbo frames) and security features, such as the introduction of Link Layer Topology Discovery (LLTD) and turning off the default behavior to allow viewing of other devices on the network.

▪ **Note**   If you are interested in learning more about the new Next Generation TCP/IP Stack introduced in Windows Vista and Windows Server 2008, visit TechNet: `https://technet.microsoft.com/en-us/network/bb545475.aspx?f=255&MSPPError=-2147217396`.

Network-Based Security

A new approach to detecting malware is to attempt to detect it before it arrives at the client. Instead of relying solely on the client device to protect itself, the network is also charged with the duty of overall network security.

Network attacks are typically restricted to fewer than ten distinct communication protocols, such as UDP, TCP, HTML, etc. Dedicated network equipment can look for viruses traversing the network.

Both solutions will analyze for the thousands of potential virus signatures, but the network device can achieve this while the virus is in transit, whereas a client-based anti-malware solution must monitor and then quarantine once the virus has landed onto the PC.

Increasingly, service providers will offer network-based solutions that allow enterprises to subscribe to a fully managed anti-malware solution. The hardware is supplied, maintained, and managed, and malware is detected, quarantined, analyzed, and reviewed by the service provider. Because this is deployed on a subscription model, this is Security as a Service.

By utilizing this type of solution, your network benefits from an "always-on," "always up-to-date" solution that cannot be disabled by the user (or by malware).

With the constant threat from malware, it is recommended that both network-based and client-based security solutions are employed, as these represent separate layers in your defense-in-depth strategy.

Identifying External Attacks

The majority of security breaches are from external attacks. If malware is attacking computers within your environment, how will you know? Most PC users will have some awareness of malware threats, through training or personal experience, but as we have seen earlier, the attacks keep being re-engineered and become more sophisticated and less easy to spot. In extreme cases, home users can become exceedingly concerned by the threat of malware and identity theft, and I have seen users stop using their computers.

In order to discuss external attacks, I will first identify the most common types of external malware that are encountered today.

The common external malware types are currently

- Firewall attacks and DDoS

- E-mail borne viruses and ransomware

- Spear phishing

- Targeted application hacking

Firewall Attacks and DDoS

We saw in Chapter 3 how important the firewall and DMZ area are in creating a physical boundary that protects your internal resources from the Internet, wherein hide unknown threats.

The primary reason for hackers to implement a firewall attack is to create a breach opening and allow ingress of specialist network traffic, which can be laden with a Trojan horse or virus. Once they have gained control of the network firewall, or a device on the inside of the network, they will be able to hide their tracks and create additional pathways into the network. Having multiple access routes is useful if a tunnel is compromised or if each vector has a different purpose. Often, when a threat is uncovered, the typical response is to close the vulnerability, whereas the correct response should be to perform a full security audit and look for other threats residing on the network.

A distributed denial-of-service attack is when a hacker uses multiple bots (distributed robotic services) to attempt a flooding of the router with more requests than it can handle. A successful DDoS can result in several possible outcomes.

- Authorized users being unable to access resources

- Creation of a smokescreen for the "real" or "secondary" attack

- Failure of one or more networking components

- Compromise of the networking component

- Opening of a backdoor into the computer, allowing remote control of it.

- Loss of reputational goodwill

> ■ **Note** Bots are defined as being individual infected machines, and botnets are multiple bots working together. Bots, when used for hacking purposes, are manipulated by the hacker. Bots can be used to issue spam on a near-continuous basis. The Rustock spamming botnet operated for five years between 2006 and 2011 and infected an estimated 2.4 million computers worldwide.

E-mail-Borne Viruses and Ransomware

We have all encountered e-mail-borne viruses with attachments that entice us to open them, thereby unleashing the payload to infect our computers. This will continue and become more effective.

We have already covered file based attachments in Chapter 1 and again in Chapter 3. In all business environments, unknown attachments within e-mails should be sandboxed (typically, automatically placed in a virtualized environment), until they have been checked and, if safe, released. Methods to evade detection, such as encrypting or compressing, should also result in the files being prevented from traversing within the internal e-mail system.

Because e-mail-borne viruses are one of the oldest and most well-known methods of attack, ensuring that your users remain well-trained and vigilant, coupled with up-to-date virus scanning software, should reduce the incidence rate of any e-mail virus.

Should you fall foul of an e-mail virus in which you open an infected file, it is likely that the payload will be some form of ransomware. This method of attack has gained huge success in recent years, because it encrypts your personal files and then holds you ransom until you pay the perpetrator. The concept has been very effective and financially successful, with the original ransomware viruses and their derivatives. Cryptolocker, discovered in late 2013, reportedly extorted a staggering $30 million in the first three months after release. Even if this is a wild exaggeration, it still shows that a lot of money is being made.

It is worth mentioning how you can identify whether you have been infected by ransomware. Ransomware requires an executable to deliver its payload, and, therefore, the most common method is to hide within a downloaded Torrent file.

Once infected, the virus will associate itself with system and application file extensions, so that when you try to open an application, for example, Word or Excel, the virus will display a custom pop dialog that informs you of its malicious action. Most ransomware viruses will encrypt your personal files and request that you pay a ransom in Bitcoin to have your files decrypted. The virus is normally time-bombed, to create urgency, so that the victim panics and makes prompt payment. Often, once payment has been received, the files are either not decrypted, or, if they are, the virus may lay dormant and resurface for another payment six months later.

An example of the dialog screen from the PClock2 ransomware is shown in Figure 4-3.

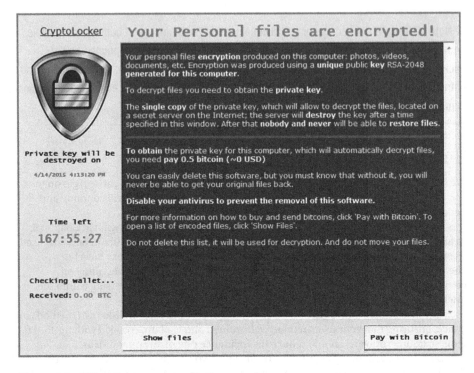

Figure 4-3. *PClock2 ransomware display message*

The existence of the PClock2 virus can be established by checking the registry for the presence of the following key:

```
[HKEY_CURRENT_USER\Software\Microsoft\Windows\CurrentVersion\Run\]
"wincl" = "%APPDATA%\WinDsk\windsk.exe"
```

The virus will also store malware files locally in the following locations:

- %APPDATA%\WinDsk\windsk.exe: The malware executable
- %APPDATA%\WinDsk\windskwp.jpg: The custom wallpaper generated by the malware
- %DESKTOP%\CryptoLocker.lnk: A shortcut to the malware executable
- %USERPROFILE%\enc_files.txt: List of encrypted files

After infection, the machine is unusable, until the virus is removed. This may be achieved using a decrypter tool available from your antivirus vendor.

Ransomware that has already been released should be detected by your anti-malware software, but due to the lucrative nature of this attack, it is likely that significant effort will be invested to create new variants of ransomware and make them harder to detect before they release their payload.

The suggested defense against this type of malware is to back up regularly (onto media stored disconnected from the PC) and remain vigilant to all executable files. Enterprise machines should not be able to accidentally activate any ransomware executables, especially if they are using a modern operating system with UAC enabled. Users of older systems are particularly at risk.

Spear Phishing

One method of increasing the effectiveness of e-mail attacks is known as spear phishing. This is typically an e-mail-borne phishing attack that has been customized with your information, so that it appears legitimate. For readers of this book, this may not be a huge threat, but for inexperienced users, this type of targeted, specific scam whereby the sender e-mail address is also impersonated, the e-mail content can become even more compelling to the recipient who knows the purported sender.

With the explosion of personal and corporate information available on social media and public sites such as LinkedIn, it is now even easier to connect pieces of the jigsaw and make a previously laughable spam e-mail become entirely credible.

Targeted Application Hacking

On October 21, 2015, UK telecommunications provider TalkTalk was successfully hacked, with the loss of customer data. Once the breach was investigated, a database containing 4 million records, of approximately 157,000 customers, including names, addresses, and bank account details, had been accessed.

The perpetrators e-mailed several TalkTalk employees with ransom demands and included some proof of the stolen cache of data.

The attackers were apprehended in November and December 2015, whereupon more details of the breach become known. One of the hackers was a 15-year-old boy from Northern Ireland who had used an SQL injection attack on a database maintained in a third-party call center. Preceding the theft, the hacker used a DDoS attack that distracted TalkTalk's security team.

During the trial of the hackers in November 2016, TalkTalk admitted that it was not aware that the hacked web server contained vulnerable web pages that could be used to access the membership database. The company also confirmed that it was not aware that the database software was outdated and not supported by Microsoft.

The incident cost TalkTalk an estimated $75 million and the loss of 95,000 customers, as well as a sharp drop in its share price. The criminal told magistrates, "I was just showing off to my mates."

The SQL injection attack method in the TalkTalk breach had been discovered more than ten years ago, and a patch was available. It is important to review all applications for vulnerabilities and take steps to ensure that services provided by third-party contractors are also compliant with your security measures.

Another external attack on the database of an adult dating service, "Friend Finder Network," reportedly exposed between 340 million and 412 million accounts, e-mail addresses, and passwords from its web sites, dumping them on the black market. No details of how the actual hackers gained access to the data was available at the time of writing.

It is not just the enterprise-grade database applications that are at risk of attack. In the last ten years, there have been severe vulnerabilities discovered in popular add-ons, including Oracle Java, Adobe Reader, and Adobe Flash. Unless PCs and their applications are regularly updated, they are vulnerable to exploit kits.

Identifying Internal Attacks

An internal attack refers to a malicious activity that seeks to disrupt the computer systems from within the workplace. This could be directly from a member of staff, a contractor, or a visitor. The action may be deliberate or accidental.

During a recent security briefing, the consensus was that human error opens more doors to hackers than technical shortcomings, resulting in a permeable perimeter that is a constant challenge to police. Insider threats remain a significant cyber risk to organizations, with a quarter of all malware attacks originating from the inside.

Trusted employees often require access to critical systems and data, to perform their role within the work environment. The employer has a legal duty to protect the business from any form of fraud or malicious activity. In light of this and other legislation (such as the US Sarbanes-Oxley Act of 2002), it is essential that careful consideration be given to how much scope each role within the workplace is given to individual employees.

A disgruntled employee can cause significant financial and reputational damage through the theft of sensitive data and intellectual property when they leave, and often the damage is not discovered for several months.

Members of staff with specific IT knowledge and access may cause destructive cyber damage by facilitating, or launching, an attack to disrupt or degrade critical services or wipe data from the organization's network.

Accidental damage can also occur by staff, for example, if an employee inadvertently infects the network with a virus.

Other examples of accidental damage include

- Clicking on a phishing e-mail

- Plugging an infected USB into a computer

- Ignoring security procedures

- Allowing unauthorized use of company devices

- Downloading unsafe content from the Internet

Social engineering is a growing threat. It is akin to the tactics employed by World War II spies, and there was a need to curtail all idle talk in case a spy was listening. Posters similar to the one shown in Figure 4-4 would remind you to keep your daily activities to yourself.

"Keep it under your hat!"

CARELESS TALK COSTS LIVES

G-2 V1 ARMY CORPS

Figure 4-4. *World War II poster aimed at curbing information leakage*

Social engineering is one of the easiest methods by which to obtain sensitive information about an enterprise. Individuals, such as reception staff or junior employees, are regularly targeted and can unwittingly provide access to the network or carry out instructions in good faith that benefit the fraudster. Common (and successful) examples of social engineering include the following:

- Phishing scams to obtain personal information, such as names, addresses, and Social Security numbers

- URL link shorteners to obfuscate malicious links that redirect users to suspicious web sites

- Pretexting, whereby an attacker focuses on creating a good pretext, such as a fabricated scenario, to try and steal information or scam their victim into allowing entry into the building

- Baiting can be used to spread hidden malware by distributing free or gifted USB sticks to staff that contain a virus. A similar method is to leave USB sticks plugged into a meeting room PC and wait for it to be turned on and then capture and broadcast the credentials, using keylogging malware.

- Tailgating is very common and relatively easy to pull off, especially in a large organization. Someone without the proper authentication follows an employee into a restricted area, leaves a USB in an unattended computer, and then walks out.

There are many ways to reduce the overall cyber risk to an organization, which will form part of your security policy documentation and should be included in employee employment contracts and contractor agreements.

The technological bar required to create sophisticated malware is becoming higher, but some malware is now obtainable to buy directly from the Dark Web. If malware eventually becomes less effective, it is possible that hackers and fraudsters will target physical access into an organization, as this may become the easiest entry vector.

Another very high-profile cyber attack occurred in July–August 2015 on the databases of the online dating service offered by Ashley Madison. This hack is believed to have been the result of an internal breach and emphasizes the importance of the internal threat. Ashley Madison claimed to have an international membership of 37.6 million, and details of this membership was stolen and subsequently made public. It was one of the largest file ransomware attacks.

Because of the highly sensitive nature of the data stolen and publicly released, the fallout following the breach included suicides, lost employment, and families and reputations destroyed. The hackers have never been identified, but many industry experts believe the breach bore the signs of an insider job.

Historically, companies have approached cyber security from a cost-benefit perspective. It is often thought cheaper to deal with the fallout from a breach. However, when the risk of a security leak is the size of Ashley Madison or AdultFriendFinder, security must take priority at any cost.

The need for a positive and proactive security culture that is alert and responsive to the threat posed by the various forms of espionage is extremely important in this modern age.

Summary

Although attacks sponsored by nation-states and terrorist groups and huge leaks of personal data make the headlines, they actually make up a very small minority of the total number of breaches. The main focus for malware today and in the near future is to steal your money. Ransomware is the biggest current security threat to the computer user at home and at work.

As the technical aspects of cyber warfare continue to rise, we will see more social engineering techniques deployed that aim to steal identity and gain the access that criminals desire.

In the next chapter, you will see how to assess PCs for security vulnerabilities and use tools to help remove malware, once your device is infected.

CHAPTER 5

External Malware and Virus Resources

There are few experiences worse than your PC being infected by malware. Normal reactions to being struck with a virus include shock, panic, and fear. Depending on where personal data, such as family photos, correspondence, and downloaded files is located, your level of anxiety can become extreme.

Help is at hand, and there are many options available to you to protect and recover your machine from the grip of malware.

In this chapter, you will learn not to panic and to approach the cleanup task in a methodical and measured way that should help give you the best chance to make a full recovery.

Chapter Goal   How the reader can use the tools and utilities available from Windows and third parties that can help identify and remove malware from a PC.

---

1. Malware Protection Center

2. Microsoft Baseline Security Analyzer

3. Windows Defender

4. Third-Party Malware and Malware Removal Tools in Depth

5. Windows Defender Advanced Threat Protection

Malware Protection Center

All current versions of Windows can access the security software offered by the Malware Protection Center at www.microsoft.com/en-us/security/portal/mmpc/default.aspx. Microsoft has curated a dedicate security portal for business and consumer Windows users. You should bookmark the web site and take some time to review the various tools and resources that are available and which could help restore your PC to good health following a malware attack.

© Andrew Bettany and Mike Halsey 2017
A. Bettany and M. Halsey, *Windows Virus and Malware Troubleshooting*,
DOI 10.1007/978-1-4842-2607-0_5

Because the resources are maintained online, you can be assured that they are accessible and up to date, regardless of a malware infection on your device. On the Malware Protection Center, there are three key resources areas: Get updates, for security software; Get protected, to download security software; and Get Microsoft support, to explore support options, as shown in Figure 5-1.

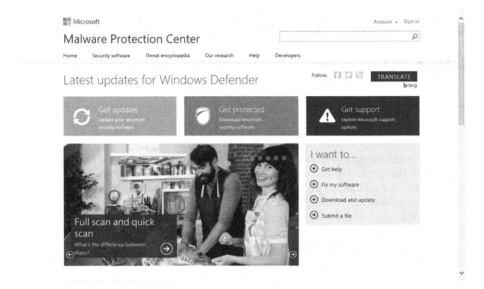

Figure 5-1. *Microsoft online Malware Protection Center*

Get Updates for Security Software

Within the update section, Microsoft provides step-by-step guidance on how you can update your Microsoft anti-malware and anti-spyware software. There are useful links for obtaining the security software and on how to troubleshoot Windows Update if it stops working. Within the advanced troubleshooting area, there is also a guide showing you how to mitigate malware that prevents you from using Windows Update and a list of potential error codes that your security software can issue.

Considerations that may prevent Windows Update from obtaining the latest anti-malware signatures covered in the resource pages include

- Freeing up space on your PC, to allow for updates to be saved

- Updating your security software and running a full scan

- Updating vulnerable software with the latest patches and service packs

- Using the Microsoft Safety Scanner or Windows Defender Offline to clean malware from your device

- Viewing the extensive encyclopedia for known malware and any special instructions on removal and cleanup.

- How to restore your PC from a backup

From the portal, you can download antivirus and anti-spyware updates for the following supported security applications:

- Microsoft Security Essentials

- Windows Defender in Windows 8.1 and Windows 10

- Windows Defender in Windows 7 and Windows Vista

- Microsoft Diagnostics and Recovery Toolset (DaRT)

- Forefront Client Security

- Forefront Server Security

- Forefront Endpoint Protection

- System Center 2012 Configuration Manager

- System Center 2012 Endpoint Protection

- Windows Intune

To check that you have the most up-to-date version of your anti-malware software, you should navigate to the help or settings menu and select About, which will provide the current versioning details, as shown in Figure 5-2, for Windows Defender.

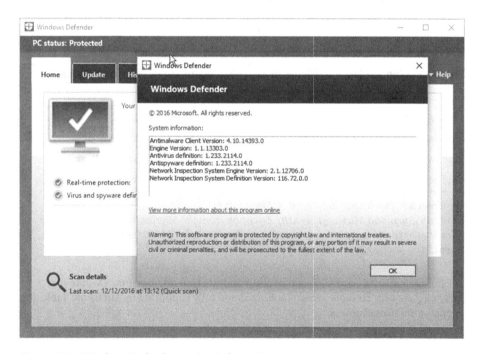

Figure 5-2. *Windows Defender version information*

Download Security Software

When you click the Get protected link on the Malware Protection Center portal, you are provided with a matrix of options that relate to the security software that is available, including the following:

- Microsoft Security Essentials

- Windows Defender

- Malicious Software Removal Tool

- Safety Scanner

- Windows Intune

- Windows Defender Online

- Microsoft Diagnostics and Recovery Toolset (DaRT)

- System Center 2012 Endpoint Protection

Microsoft provides free client protection against malware and other threats, by offering Windows Defender, which is built into Windows 8.1 and Windows 10. Support is still available for Windows 7 and Windows Vista through the Microsoft Security Essentials package. Both tools work the same to protect you from malware.

The current available client support against malware is summarized in Table 5-1.

Table 5-1. *Microsoft Security Software*

Client Operating System	Microsoft Security Essentials	Windows Defender
Windows XP*	N/A	N/A
Windows Vista	Free**	N/A
Windows 7	Free**	N/A
Windows 8.1	N/A	Free, Built-in
Windows 10	N/A	Free, Built-in

*Windows XP is no longer supported by Microsoft
**You can download Microsoft Security Essentials from the Microsoft Security Essentials web site at https://support.microsoft.com/en-us/help/14210/security-essentials-download.

Both Microsoft Security Essentials and Windows Defender are free. Despite the price, they are very credible security solutions and fully supported by Microsoft. Table 5-2 compares the two solutions.

Table 5-2. *Comparing Windows Defender and Microsoft Security Essentials*

Feature	Microsoft Security Essentials: Windows Vista, Windows 7	Windows Defender: Windows 8, Windows RT, Windows 8.1, Windows RT 8.1, Windows 10
Real-time protection against spyware, viruses, rootkits, and other malicious software	X	X
Online system scanning and cleaning	X	X
Dynamic signature service	X	X
Offline system scanning and cleaning	X	X
Enhanced protection against rootkits		X

You will notice that Windows XP does not have a Microsoft-supported anti-malware solution. As of April 8, 2014, technical support for Windows XP stopped including updates that help protect Windows XP PCs against attack.

Get Microsoft Support

The final option on the Malware Protection Center portal allows you to seek specialist help from the various Microsoft support channels in relation to Windows security.

On the support page, you can search for help, drill down to a specific product, and locate product support. You can also submit questions to the community of Microsoft experts, by clicking the Ask the Community option.

Once on the community page, you can fine-tune the resources available, by selecting the version of Windows and the category, such as virus and malware, and the type of solution, from the available Microsoft security solutions. Finally, select the type of help you require, such as the scanning, detecting, and removing threats, and click Apply. An example of community search results relating to viruses and malware is shown in Figure 5-3.

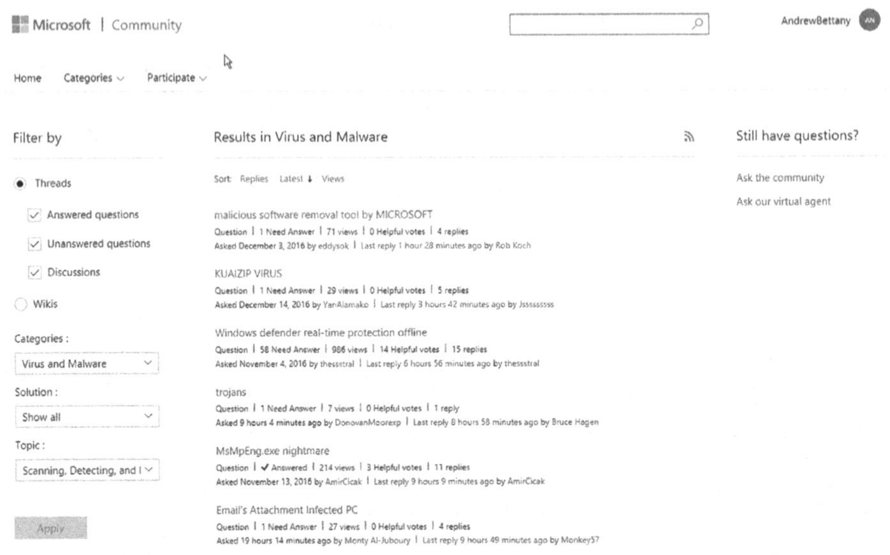

Figure 5-3. *Detailed help from Microsoft Community*

One of the biggest hindrances to cleaning up after a malware attack is that most users are unaware of the help and support that Microsoft and other security vendors provide. This information has to be shared, so that the fear of malware, and any guilt, panic, and shame felt following an attack, can be alleviated.

If you want to keep up to date with the very latest security trends and methods to detect and thwart malware attacks, you should regularly download your preferred security vendor's newsletter. For Microsoft, you can read the *Microsoft Security Intelligence Report*, shown in Figure 5-4, which is produced twice a year and is available from www.microsoft.com/security/sir/default.aspx.

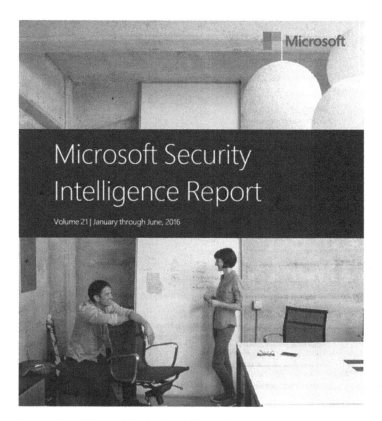

Figure 5-4. *Microsoft Security Intelligence Report*

Microsoft Baseline Security Analyzer

The Microsoft Baseline Security Analyzer (MBSA) has been available for a number of years across many versions of Windows. The MBSA tool tries to identify security vulnerabilities on your system.

I have found that despite the MBSA being around for a very long time, only a few users are aware of this free tool. MBSA 2.3 is the current version, and it works with Windows 8.1 and previous versions of Windows. It can be downloaded from www.microsoft.com/en-gb/download/details.aspx?id=7558.

After downloading the MBSA file (1.7MB), you should install it and then launch the analyzer. MBSA allows you to choose to scan a single machine, a range of IP addresses, or to review an existing security scan report.

If you check for security updates, which is recommended, MBSA must first download the latest security update information from Microsoft, which may take up to ten minutes. The tool will then automatically continue with the security scan, and the finished summary, shown in Figure 5-5, will be presented and can be saved or printed.

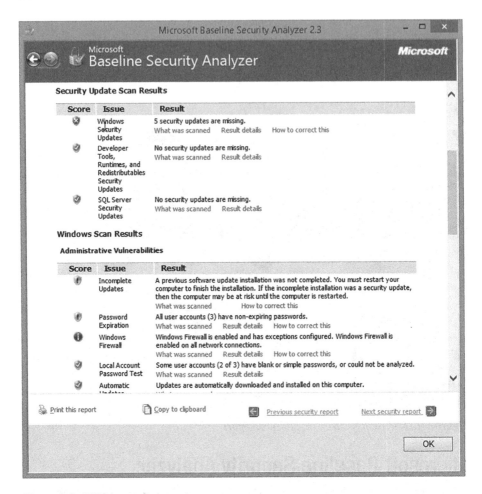

Figure 5-5. *MBSA security report*

The tool produces a user-friendly report that can be used to benchmark devices and confirm that your system is not missing patches and common security vulnerabilities. The majority of issues MBSA identifies relate to missing security patches and others relating to user accounts. You should review the findings and implement the recommendations.

■ **Note** You can find more information about MBSA at `https://technet.microsoft.com/en-us/security/cc184924.aspx`.

Windows Defender

Windows Defender was originally known as Microsoft AntiSpyware and was eventually included with Windows Vista and Windows 7.

Windows Defender offers every Windows user a perfectly good anti-malware package at an affordable price: free. If you have no loyalty to another third-party tool, save your money and stay with the official bundled anti-malware solution that is recommended and integrated into the operating system that it is trying to protect.

Windows Defender runs as a background process (`MsMpEng.exe`) and monitors your system continuously by default. You should, however, take the opportunity to check that it is running and also whether automatic updating of the virus and spyware definitions are up to date, as shown in Figure 5-6. Start Windows Defender by typing "defender" into the Search Windows box and select Windows Defender.

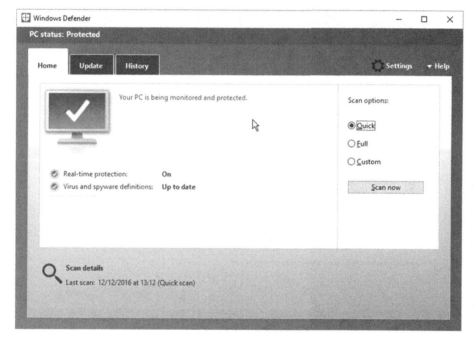

Figure 5-6. *Windows Defender Home screen*

Windows Defender should display a green bar with the title "PC status: Protected." If it displays a red bar and "PC status: At risk," it is likely that someone has turned off real-time protection, cloud-based protection, or that malware may have infected your PC. To restore the protected status, click the Turn On button on the Windows Defender Home tab or use the following steps:

1. Open Settings

2. Update & security

3. Windows Defender

4. Turn on Real-time protection

5. Turn on Cloud-based protection

6. Open Windows Defender and perform a Quick Scan

If Windows Defender finds malware or a potentially harmful or suspicious file, it will immediately move it to quarantine, where it is safe from you or from other malware accessing it.

To view any malware that has been detected, you can click the History tab within Windows Defender, select All detected items, and click View details. The list of files will appear in the table following, as shown in Figure 5-7.

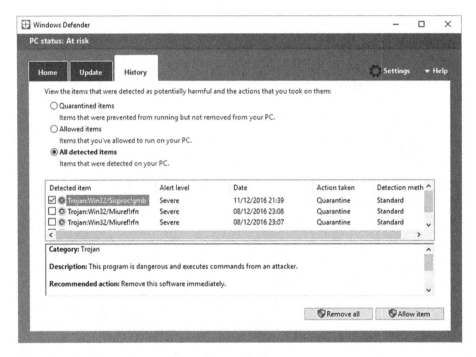

Figure 5-7. *Malware detected by Windows Defender*

If you have harmful files that have been detected, you should maximize the Windows Defender screen, then you can see the file name and location path belonging to the malware. At the bottom of the detected file information is a Get more information about this item online link that will direct you to a page within the Microsoft Malware Protection Center that provides information, technical data, and removal advice relating to the item, as shown in Figure 5-8.

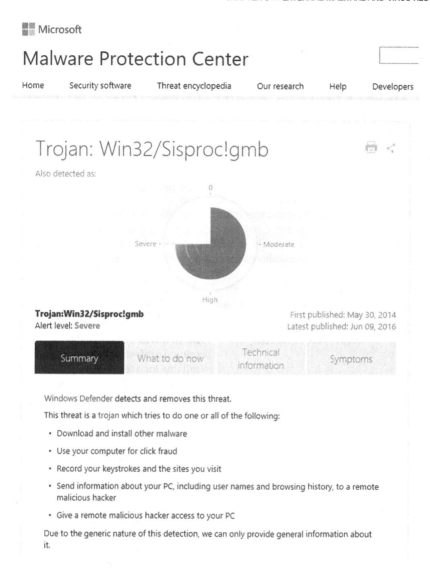

Figure 5-8. *Detailed malware information*

If the files that Windows Defender detects as malware are, in fact, safe, this is known as a false positive. You can use the Add an exclusion setting within the Windows Defender settings to exclude monitoring specific files and areas on your device, such as excluding files, folders, file extensions, and processes, including .exe program files.

Windows Defender is normally updated through Windows Update, which is enabled by default, and if this is disabled, Windows will provide you with a warning that your system is not protected.

It is worth mentioning that some users may never encounter malware, while for others, it may be a constant battle. Allowing Windows to maintain a continual watch over your system will certainly help to mitigate the ever-present threat of malware.

Third-Party Malware and Malware Removal Tools in Depth

Antivirus protection is absolutely necessary if your device is connected to the outside world, such as the Internet, e-mail system, or even external media such as CDs and USB drives.

You have already seen that there are many antivirus packages available. Some are free and others follow a monthly or annual subscription payment model.

Which should you choose? I recommend the built-in Microsoft anti-malware solutions that are discussed throughout this book, but there are others that you should consider.

I have chosen some third-party tools, shown in Table 5-3, based on their longevity and consistency in scoring well in antivirus scanning tests over the last few years.

Table 5-3. *Selection of Third-Party Tools*

Tool	URL	Description
AVG Antivirus FREE	`http://free.avg.com`	This tool is free but includes an optional professional version available for a fee. AVG has long been considered one of the best free anti-malware packages for Windows 7 and later operating systems. Among its key features, it stops viruses, spyware, and other malware; warns against unsafe web links; blocks dangerous e-mail attachments; and scans quickly and quietly.
Norton Security	`www.symantec.com`	Norton was an early pioneer in providing malware scanning for Windows, and it now offers a comprehensive suite of tools. Choose the most appropriate suite from an easy-to-view feature table. The entry-level product, Norton Antivirus Basic, includes the following features: defense against viruses, spyware, malware, phishing, software vulnerabilities, and other online threats and safeguards to protect your identity and online transactions.

(continued)

Table 5-3. (*continued*)

Tool	URL	Description
Trend Micro Antivirus+ Security	www.trendmicro.com	A highly effective antivirus package. No free layer, but it contains many features, including protection against ransomware, the ability to block 250 million+ daily threats, and safeguards against e-mail scams.
Kaspersky Anti-Virus	http://usa.kaspersky.com	Kaspersky is highly regarded among loyal users, who post positive reviews and cover the standard features to protect your PC, including protection against viruses, spyware, and more, without performance degradation, and easy, simple online controls.

In addition to these third-party tools available, there are also some additional tools that Microsoft maintains to help you recover from a malware attack, such as a virus, rootkit, or ransomware.

These tools can be found in the Malware Protection Center, covered earlier in this chapter, and they are summarized following.

Malicious Software Removal Tool

This tool is an essential first action when you believe your device is infected, and your current anti-malware solution has been ineffective. You can download the standalone Malicious Software Removal Tool (MSRT) from the Malware Protection Center or directly, using the following URL: www.microsoft.com/en-us/download/malicious-software-removal-tool-details.aspx.

After downloading the MSRT file (approx. 45MB), you install the application and allow the tool to scan your device. The tool is able to detect and remove the most prevalent malware and allows three levels of scans, as shown in Figure 5-9.

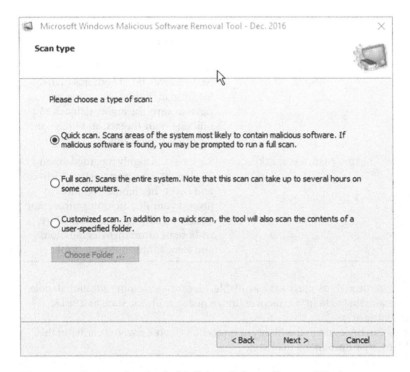

Figure 5-9. *Scan options in the Malicious Software Removal Tool*

Once started, the tool will scan your PC and search and attempt to remove any infected files it can find. The tool is fast, taking only a couple of minutes to complete, and provides you with a detailed report detailing the scan results.

The MSRT is updated monthly, on the second Tuesday of each month, and you should use the latest version available. The current version includes detection and removal support for well-known and prevalent malware, including Blaster, Sasser, and Mydoom.

Windows Defender Offline

This tool is a powerful offline scanning tool you boot to from Windows 10, or via CD, DVD, or USB flash drive for other versions of Windows. It runs before your operating system boots and, therefore, provides a clean trusted environment in which to scan your system for malware, including rootkits.

As Windows Defender Offline is built into Windows 10, it requires no additional media in order to perform and is extremely useful if your device has a rootkit or your PC is already infected and malware prevents you from scanning or removing the virus by using your installed anti-malware software or the MSRT.

If you suspect your PC has malware, you can start a Windows Defender Offline scan from Windows Defender Settings, by following these steps:

1. Log on to Windows 10 using administrative credentials

2. Open Settings

3. Select Update & security

4. Select Windows Defender

5. Click Scan Offline

Once you click Scan Offline, the Windows Defender Offline tool will log you out from Windows and then restart the PC and boot to the Windows Defender Offline console and automatically perform a quick scan of your PC, as shown in Figure 5-10.

Figure 5-10. *Windows Defender Offline Quick scan*

Once complete, the tool will exit and reboot Windows. To view the Windows Defender Offline scan results, you should follow these steps:

1. Log on to Windows 10 using administrative credentials

2. Open Windows Defender

3. Click the History tab

4.   Select the All detected items

5.   Click View Details

Any items detected by Windows Defender Offline will be listed as Offline in the Detection method column.

If you are using Windows 7, you will have to download Windows Defender Offline and create a bootable CD, DVD, or USB flash drive and then manually restart your PC, using the Windows Defender Offline media.

You can download the Windows Defender Offline (`mssstool32exe` or `mssstool64.exe`) tool directly from the Malware Protection Center or via the following URL: `https://support.microsoft.com/en-us/help/17466/windows-defender-offline-help-protect-my-pc`.

It is recommended that you only download the tool at the point you need it, because the tool is regularly maintained by Microsoft to contain the most up-to-date signature definitions.

Microsoft Safety Scanner

Microsoft Safety Scanner is another antivirus tool that is a standalone virus and malware scanner that runs inside Windows. It was built for Windows 7 and later versions and has been replaced by the Malicious Software Removal Tool, although both tools are still available to download the from the Malware Protection Center. A direct download is available via `www.microsoft.com/security/scanner`.

The downloaded file (`Msert.exe`) is quite large, being 140MB, and is an on-demand scanner that may be useful if your current antivirus solution has been disabled. Because of the volatile nature of malware, the Microsoft Safety Scanner is designed to run inside Windows and expires ten days following the download. Each time you download the tool, the most up-to-date anti-malware definitions are included.

When you run the downloaded anti-malware signature package, Microsoft Safety Scanner, as shown in Figure 5-11, behaves in a near-identical manner to the Malicious Software Removal Tool that we saw earlier, in that the scan is performed while Windows is running, and it will scan and remove viruses, spyware, and other potentially unwanted programs (PuPs).

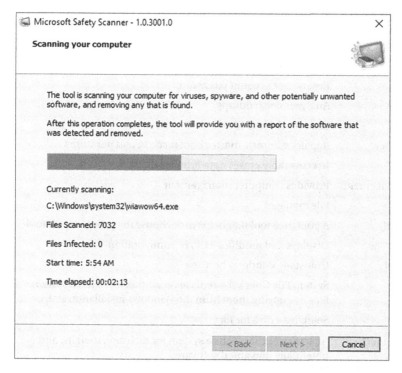

Figure 5-11. *Microsoft Safety Scanner*

Diagnostics and Recovery Toolset (DaRT)

The Microsoft Diagnostics and Recovery Toolset provides a rich set of tools to help you troubleshoot and repair system failures, including malware hunting, and is available in 11 different languages.

You can download the DaRT from the Malware Protection Center or directly via the following URL: https://technet.microsoft.com/en-us/windows/hh826071.aspx.

The DaRT tools are available to enterprises for diagnosing an offline copy of Microsoft Windows, since Microsoft acquired the ERD Commander tools from Winternals in 2006. The bootable recovery tools that are contained on the CD, DVD, or USB flash drive you create with DaRT have been extended over the years and now include many tools, as listed in Table 5-4.

Table 5-4. *DaRT Tools*

DaRT Tool	Description
Registry editor	Edits Windows Registry
Locksmith	Resets user account password
Crash Analyzer	Analyzes crash dumps
File Restore	Restores deleted files
Disk Commander	Repairs volumes, master boot records, and partitions
Disk Wipe	Irrecoverably erases data from hard disk
Computer Management	Provides computer management
Explorer	File manager
Solution Wizard	A guidance tool that helps user choose the proper repair tool
TCP/IP Config	Displays and modifies TCP/IP configuration
Hotfix Uninstall	Uninstalls Windows hotfixes
SFC Scan	System File Checker—replaces corrupted or deleted system files by copying them from the Windows installation source
Search	Searches a disk for files
Windows Defender*	An antivirus that scans a system for malware, rootkits, and potentially unwanted software

Not available in DaRT 10

One of the main uses for DaRT is the Defender tool, shown in Figure 5-12 with its other tools, which allows you to hunt for malware while Windows is offline. This tool is now included directly in Windows 10 and is not available in DaRT 10.

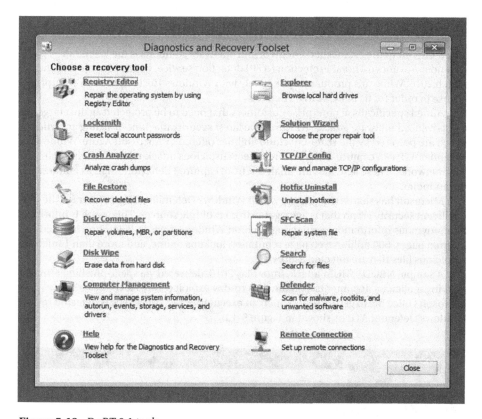

Figure 5-12. *DaRT 8.1 tools*

The DaRT 10 toolset is the current version and should be used for Windows 10, whereas earlier versions of DaRT (DaRT 7, DaRT 8, and DaRT 8.1, together with their service packs) should be used for prior versions of Windows.

It is now recommended that for older devices, the Microsoft Diagnostics and Recovery Toolset (DaRT) Defender tool should not now be used, because the DaRT tools are infrequently updated. Users are advised to use the Windows Defender Offline (WDO) protection image for malware detection and removal.

DaRT 10 is a part of the Microsoft Desktop Optimization Pack (MDOP), and the MDOP is only available to enterprises that own a current Microsoft Software Assurance license. If you believe you have Microsoft Software Assurance or want to find more information about acquiring MDOP, visit the site at https://go.microsoft.com/fwlink/?LinkId=322049.

Windows Defender Advanced Threat Protection

A new entrant to the established lineup of anti-malware solutions is the Windows Defender Advanced Threat Protection (ATP) detection service, which was released in March 2016. While this product ships natively with Windows 10, it requires an enterprise license in order for its benefits to be derived.

Aimed specifically at enterprise customers that need to be protected against targeted and advanced malware attacks, ATP uses the latest security machine-learning analytics, which are powered by the scale-out cloud abilities offered by Microsoft Azure. Windows Defender ATP can capture, analyze, and detect suspicious attack-related activities on your networks. These activities are analyzed from captured behavioral signals emitted at the endpoint.

Microsoft has shared the scale at which Windows Defender ATP can leverage the intelligent security graph that is aggregated from multiple sources. This graph is informed by anonymous information connecting 1 billion Windows devices, 2.5 trillion indexed Internet pages, 600 million web page reputation lookups online, and more than 1 million suspicious files that are infected every day.

A sample NEODYMIUM attack, from May 2016, delivered via spear-phishing e-mails carrying malicious documents, contained zero-day exploit code that could cause a Microsoft Office file to generate and open an executable file. This attack is detected by Windows Defender ATP, as shown in Figure 5-13.

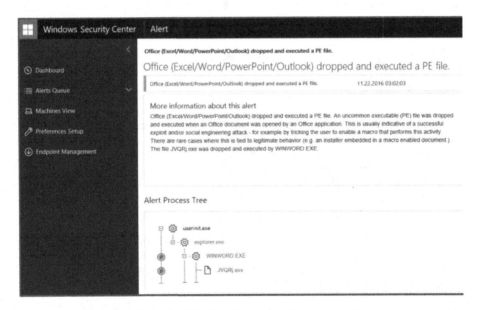

Figure 5-13. *Windows Defender ATP showing an alert for an exploit*

Windows Defender ATP is still a very new development, but it is clear to see that Microsoft has decided to move the detection and analysis of malware to the cloud, in order to reduce the time that any new potentially harmful malware is left undetected and, therefore, able to infect Windows 10 devices. Windows Defender ATP works in conjunction with the built-in Windows Defender agent to perform capabilities such as device local file scanning.

You can currently download a trial of Windows Defender ATP to be used on any of the following editions of Windows 10: Windows 10 Enterprise, Windows 10 Education, Windows 10 Pro, and Windows 10 Pro Education.

Enterprises should contact their Windows solution provider to discuss the pricing for the Microsoft Secure Productive Enterprise E3/E5 license required to deploy the product. You can sign up for a trial and gain more information via `www.microsoft.com/en-us/WindowsForBusiness/windows-atp`.

Summary

If you are using a modern version of Microsoft Windows, such as 7, 8.1, or 10, you are better protected from malware than with previous versions of Windows. This protection comes with some caveats, which include using the default Windows Defender and user account control settings and being vigilant when using e-mail and the Web, especially if any Torrent or Dark Web downloads are on your machine.

To ultimately protect your personal files from malware, you should consider storing a backup of your files, separate from your computer. I recommend a physically separate backup. The cloud is a great convenience to us, but it offers little protection against a ransomware attack, which can spread within minutes to every file you have access to.

Sometimes malware-killer applications and virus cleaners won't work. Maybe your system is too badly infected or has multiple instances of malware. Thankfully, with Windows 10, the process of resetting your PC is very simple and efficient and can be a very quick and simple way to rid a device of malware.

The final piece of the jigsaw following eradication of malware is to learn from the experience. Review how the attack occurred, where the vulnerably existed, and how you can reduce the likelihood of a repeat attack.

If malware does strike, and you cannot clean your machine using the tools highlighted in this chapter, you may have to resort to manually cleaning the infection. This will be covered in the next chapter and will require you to roll up your sleeves and go malware hunting!

■ ■ ■

CHAPTER 6

Manually Removing Malware

So far in this book, we've detailed the malware threats we all face on a day-to-day basis, the tools available for defending against, identifying, and removing malware, and the services and resources available to help you in these tasks.

It seems then that the logical way to bind all of this together is to walk through, step by step, the processes involved in identifying and safely removing malware on an infected PC.

In this case, we'll examine "zero-day" malware, the term used to describe new or newly discovered malware that the antivirus vendors haven't yet developed an automatic repair tool for.

You'll be delighted to hear, then, that I have deliberately infected my PC (well, a virtual machine, anyway) with a zero-day virus, so that I can show you how to remove it. In this case, I've not infected myself with anything malicious but, rather, a "test virus" that was developed by a team of security researchers at CQURE, so many thanks to them.

Manually Removing Malware

The test virus I have infected my PC with will mimic all the actions of a regular virus. It's appeared as an innocuous file, but it's already downloaded additional payloads from a hidden server, embedded itself in my start-up processes and the Windows Registry, and, as I write this, it's looking around for other PCs on my network that it can infect.

Step 1: Isolate the PC

That last point is very important, as malware removal becomes significantly more difficult if it's permitted to propagate and infect other PCs across your network.

Thus, disconnecting the infected PC from both the network and the Internet should always be the first step. There are many occasions on which a virus will have several running processes. These processes will perform such tasks as restarting one of the other processes, if it detects it's been terminated, or re-downloading the malware package, should it determine it's being compromised.

© Andrew Bettany and Mike Halsey 2017
A. Bettany and M. Halsey, *Windows Virus and Malware Troubleshooting*,
DOI 10.1007/978-1-4842-2607-0_6

Step 2: Identify the Running Process(es)

In order to remove malware, you must identify the processes it has running on the PC. The Windows Task Manager can help you identify a process, though it is highly unlikely that it will appear in the main Processes list. You can see the malware listed at the bottom of the Details tab in Figure 6-1. In this case, it's ~DLEE4.tmp.exe.

Name	PID	Status	Username	CPU	Memory (p...	Description
svchost.exe	916	Running	SYSTEM	00	32,896 K	Host Process for Windo...
svchost.exe	328	Running	SYSTEM	00	16,308 K	Host Process for Windo...
svchost.exe	392	Running	LOCAL SE...	00	6,104 K	Host Process for Windo...
svchost.exe	752	Running	SYSTEM	00	832 K	Host Process for Windo...
svchost.exe	1368	Running	LOCAL SE...	00	408 K	Host Process for Windo...
svchost.exe	1524	Running	LOCAL SE...	00	784 K	Host Process for Windo...
svchost.exe	1716	Running	LOCAL SE...	00	2,604 K	Host Process for Windo...
svchost.exe	1992	Running	SYSTEM	00	7,540 K	Host Process for Windo...
svchost.exe	1324	Running	SYSTEM	00	5,744 K	Host Process for Windo...
svchost.exe	2824	Running	Mike	00	3,236 K	Host Process for Windo...
svchost.exe	5684	Running	SYSTEM	00	596 K	Host Process for Windo...
svchost.exe	5960	Running	SYSTEM	00	1,432 K	Host Process for Windo...
System	4	Running	SYSTEM	00	16 K	NT Kernel & System
System Idle Process	0	Running	SYSTEM	99	4 K	Percentage of time the ...
System interrupts	-	Running	SYSTEM	00	0 K	Deferred procedure calls...
taskhostw.exe	2920	Running	Mike	00	1,288 K	Host Process for Windo...
Taskmgr.exe	6040	Running	Mike	00	8,276 K	Task Manager
VSSVC.exe	1312	Running	SYSTEM	00	536 K	Microsoft® Volume Sha...
wininit.exe	448	Running	SYSTEM	00	8 K	Windows Start-Up Appli...
winlogon.exe	480	Running	SYSTEM	00	504 K	Windows Log-on Applic...
wmpnetwk.exe	2536	Running	NETWORK...	00	956 K	Windows Media Player ...
~DLEE4.tmp.exe	4788	Running	Mike	00	1,928 K	WinlogonMalwareForm

Figure 6-1. *Task Manager can help identify malware processes*

Identifying the running process can be tricky, as you'll have no idea what the malware executable is called, that is, unless you're following removal instructions from a security vendor's web site.

The tip here is to shut down everything else on the PC, by closing it manually or from its System Tray icon. This will reduce the number of processes running on the PC.

▪ **Tip**   You can search online (on another PC or on your smartphone) for the name of the running process, to help determine if it is a legitimate app or malware, as some processes from genuine software houses can occasionally have unusual names. You can do this by right-clicking a process in the Task Manager, where a Search Online option will appear.

A better way to identify the malware process, however, is to use the Process Monitor app from the Microsoft Sysinternals Suite, http://pcs.tv/2d1CVso. You should make sure you run Process Explorer as an *administrator*.

In Figure 6-2, we can see Process Explorer running, and the malware highlighted. We can check this executable by double-clicking it, which, rather than just then being able to open the file location, as you can in the Task Manager on a right-click, makes more options available to you.

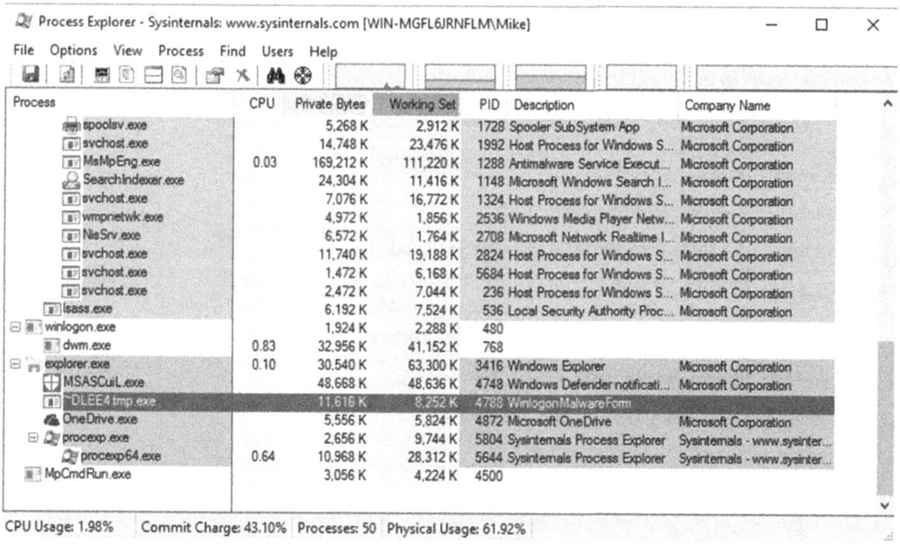

Figure 6-2. *Process Explorer is useful for identifying malware executables*

Step 3: Deactivate the Malware

We can now immediately see, in Figure 6-3, that this executable is run from the C:\Windows\Temp folder, which is highly unusual for even the most poorly written app.

Figure 6-3. *Process Explorer offers detailed information about the executable*

■ **Tip** When you double-click the malware link in Process Explorer to get information on it, make a note of the file and Registry locations for the malware, as you will need these later, when removing the malware files.

We can also see that the app is set in the Registry to start automatically whenever the PC is switched on. This is something we need to prevent, so clicking the *Explore* button next to the Autostart Location field, will open the Registry Editor at the correct point (see Figure 6-4).

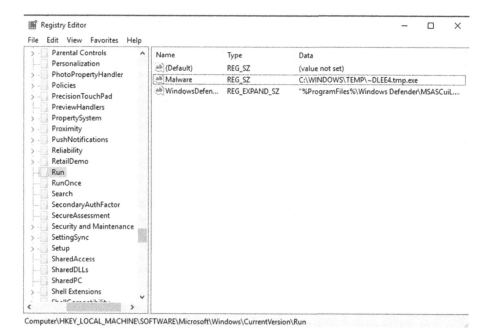

Figure 6-4. *We can see the malware entry in the Registry*

We must remove this malware startup key, so right-click it and select Delete, to remove it from the Registry.

Now we must go back to Process Explorer and shut down the executable. I've already mentioned, however, that many malware packages include secondary, or even tertiary, executables that restart the malware immediately if you shut it down. Instead, we can *Suspend* it from a right-click menu (see Figure 6-5). This may prevent other executables, if they exist, from detecting that you are attempting to remove it from the PC.

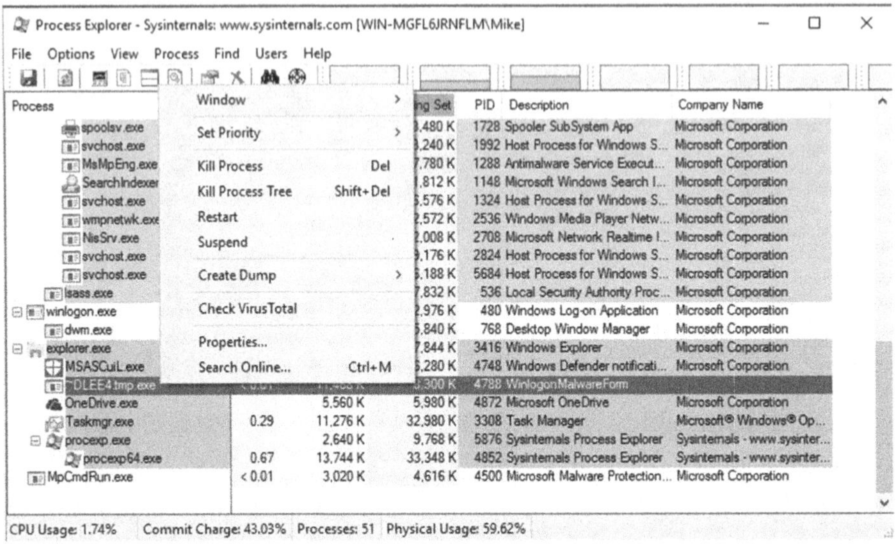

Figure 6-5. *We can kill or suspend the malware executable*

Once the malware executables have been suspended, they can all be selected together and terminated, using the Kill Process or Kill Process Tree options.

Step 4: Test the Results

We now have to restart the PC, to see if we have effectively disabled the malware. Once the PC has restarted, open Process Explorer again and check the status of the malware, should it still be running.

In this case, restarting the PC and running Process Explorer again as an administrator reveals that the malware *is* still running, albeit with a slightly different name, and the Registry entry has been re-created. We didn't get it!

The next step, then, is to open the Autoruns app from the Sysinternals Suite. Here, under the Logon tab, we can see the malware listed (see Figure 6-6). We can uncheck the malware to disable it here.

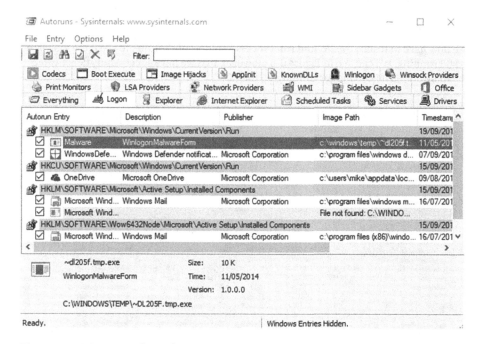

Figure 6-6. *We can see the malware autorun entry*

Because we know this malware automatically re-creates itself at sign-in, there must be something else going on. Next, we must go tab to tab and look for all the pink (not digitally signed) entries.

When we click the Winlogon tab, we can see a SampleCredentialProvider entry that's not signed but that looks legitimate (see Figure 6-7). Dynamic-link library (DLL) files are usually signed by the software developers, or by Microsoft, so we can uncheck the item to disable it, knowing that if it turns out to be important, it can be easily reenabled later, either from the desktop or from a System Restore in the Windows Recovery Environment.

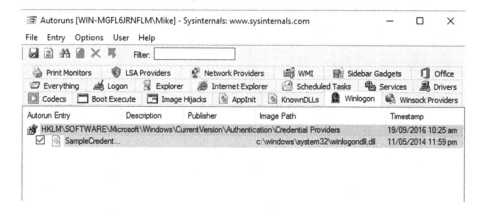

Figure 6-7. *We can see a DLL running when we sign in to the PC*

Step 5: Retest the PC

We now have to restart the PC and run Process Explorer once more, to see if the malware is still running. We can see in Figure 6-8, however, that we have successfully deactivated the malware, as it is no longer running on the PC.

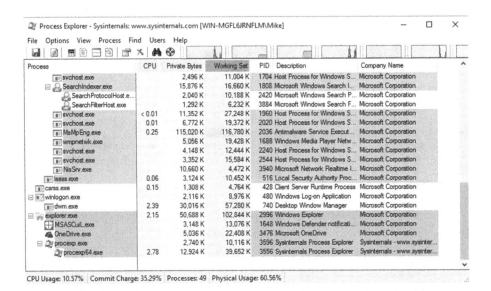

Figure 6-8. The malware is no longer running on the PC

Step 6: Remove the Malware

Now we come to the final step: to manually remove the malware files. We'll have to refer to the information we made a note of in Step 3. This is the Registry location for the malware executable and the *Windows\Temp* folder where the executables were hiding.

In this case, we can see that the Registry entry has not been re-created (Figure 6-9), but if there were something there, we'd have to delete it. You will also see an AutorunsDisabled sub-Registry key, however, and this is where our disabled key can be found.

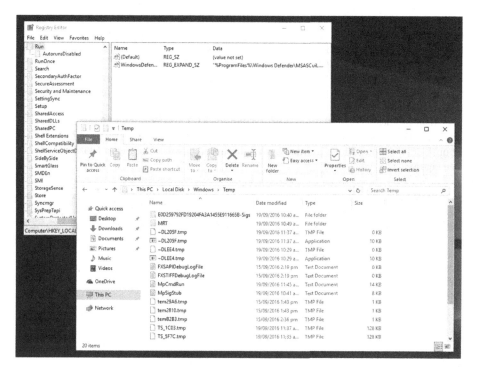

Figure 6-9. *You can manually delete the malware files and entries*

Additionally, the executable files are still residing in the *Windows\Temp* folder, and these will have to be deleted manually.

For complex malware, you can expect there to be several Registry keys and executables, and they may not all reside in the same location. This is where the information in Process Explorer is invaluable, as there may have been, as I previously mentioned, several executables running as part of the malware.

Rootkit Removal

Removing malware from an infected Windows installation is one thing, but removing the files for a rootkit from the hidden Startup partitions can pose a real challenge. This is because Windows really doesn't want you to open and view these protected partitions, and it will do everything possible to stop you, including preventing you from assigning a drive letter to the partitions in the Disk Manager.

For this task, you will require a portable OS, and I recommend a Linux distribution (here, I'm using www.ubuntu.com, but you could also use www.linuxmint.com or www.redhat.com), as these can be run from a CD or DVD nondestructively, while permitting you access to the hard disk on the host PC.

Once you have started the PC from your downloaded CD or DVD—and remember to download and create this on a non-infected PC—you can use the tools available in the Linux version, to examine the host PC's hard disk.

To do this, you may have to make the partitions visible, using a tool such as GParted, which comes with many Linux distros, but make sure you put the permissions back as you found them afterward, to minimize the risk of later reinfection by creating a potential vulnerability.

In all Windows 7 installations, and for Windows 8.1 and Windows 10 installations where the OS is installed on a PC with a 32-bit processor, or where it has been installed on a non-UEFI PC, you will see a single System Reserved partition, of about 100MB in size (see Figure 6-10).

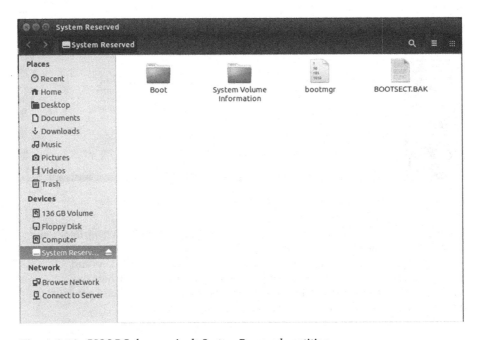

Figure 6-10. *BIOS PCs have a single System Reserved partition*

The figure shows a clean System Reserved partition. Anything additional to what you see here will more than likely be part of the rootkit. There could also be hidden or system files here that you should examine, as the rootkit tries to conceal itself.

On Windows 8.1 and Windows 10 64-bit UEFI systems, the boot partitions are more complex, with typically three separate partitions. You will see both System Reserved and EFI System partitions. These contain all the boot files needed for the PC (see Figure 6-11).

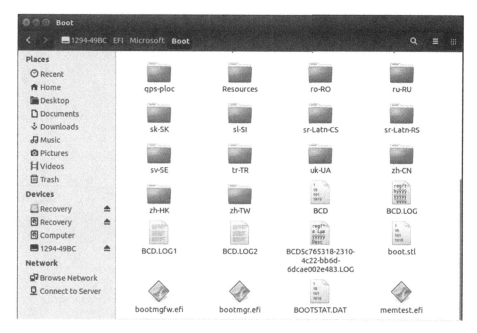

Figure 6-11. *UEFI PCs have a more complex partition structure*

Again, the figure you see here contains the contents of a clean UEFI boot partition, with the Boot Configuration Data (BCD) binary file, the Bootmgr and Memtest files, along with language folders that may be used by the boot system.

You should always be very careful when deleting files from the System Reserved partitions, as, fairly obviously, deleting the wrong file(s) can prevent you from starting the OS afterward.

Using BCDEdit

If you have had a rootkit infection on a PC, it might be prudent to check the Boot Configuration Database for signs of a payload.

You do this from a Command Prompt (Admin) window on the desktop. Typing "BCDEdit" into the Command Prompt will open the BCD Editor and display a list of all the boot options listed in the database (see Figure 6-12).

Figure 6-12. BCDEdit is used to edit the Boot Configuration Database

Have a look through the list for anything untoward that seems to point to either a rootkit file on the System Reserved partition or to a malware file on the PC itself.

If you find a suspicious entry, remember that if you delete the wrong thing, you can render the Windows installation unbootable, so use the bcdedit /delete {identifier} /cleanup command to remove it from the list.

It is very likely, in this circumstance, that the correct entry for your Windows installation will have been disabled. You can re-enable it with the command bcdedit / default {identifier}.

▓ **Note**   A full list of all the commands used with BCDEdit and details of how you can both repair and rebuild the Windows boot system can be found in my book *Windows 10 Troubleshooting* (Apress, 2016).

Summary

Malware removal can be a tricky business, with executable files, DLLs, and other files hidden and scattered about your PC. Tools such as Process Explorer and Autoruns will help significantly in this regard, but if you have been infected, you can guarantee that you won't be the only one, and a search online (from a non-infected PC, as you don't want to spread the infection across your network) can often reveal technical details that IT pros and security researchers have discovered about the malware.

In this book, I've covered everything you need to know about protecting yourself from, identifying, defending against, and removing malware. I've listed all the tools available to help with this, as well. It's crucial to remember, though, that this is only the information available *at the time this book was written*. New tools will become available; older tools might be retired; and new types of malware threats will inevitably come along to challenge researchers and security companies alike.

This means that you must be alert to the current threats, and you have to make certain (as much as humanly possible, anyway) that your PCs are secure and that the people who use them have received appropriate training in how to avoid infection.

With good PC and human strategies in place, infection should become a rare thing, and, I hope, the methods described in this last chapter won't be needed.

Index

© Andrew Bettany and Mike Halsey 2017
A. Bettany and M. Halsey, *Windows Virus and Malware Troubleshooting*,
DOI 10.1007/978-1-4842-2607-0

Get the eBook for only $4.99!

Why limit yourself?

Now you can take the weightless companion with you wherever you go and access your content on your PC, phone, tablet, or reader.

Since you've purchased this print book, we are happy to offer you the eBook for just $4.99.

Convenient and fully searchable, the PDF version enables you to easily find and copy code—or perform examples by quickly toggling between instructions and applications.

To learn more, go to http://www.apress.com/us/shop/companion or contact support@apress.com.

Printed in the United States
By Bookmasters